Tower

Air Fryer

Recipe Book UK

1000-Day Delicious, Affordable & Super-Easy Tower
Air Fryer Recipes for Beginners and Advanced Users

Caitlin Naylor

Table of Contents

Introduction 7

Fundamentals of the Tower Air Fryer..... 8

What is Tower Air Fryer?...................... 8

Benefits of Using Tower Air Fryer 8

Before First Use 10

Operating Buttons of the Towel Air Fryer. 10

Step-By-Step Air Frying 12

Air frying: 12

Cooking Tips 12

Straight from the Store...................... 13

Cleaning and Caring of Tower Air Fryer ... 13

Troubleshooting............................ 14

Type of Food with Temperature............. 14

Wiring Safety for UK Use Only 14

4-Week Diet Plan 15

Week 1.................................... 15

Week 2.................................... 15

Week 3.................................... 16

Week 4.................................... 16

Chapter 1 Breakfast Recipes.................17

Cinnamon Doughnut Holes 17

Easy Jam Doughnuts 17

Toast Sticks 17

Toaster Pastries 18

Granola Cereal 18

Raisin Granola Bars 18

Cinnamon Bagels 19

Banana-Nut Muffins.......................... 19

Scrambled Eggs 19

Hard Boiled Eggs 19

Puffed Egg Tarts 20

Hash Browns 20

Pepper & Onion Hash......................... 20

Quiche 21

Oat Blueberry Muffins 21

Baked Peaches Oatmeal 21

Glazed Cinnamon Rolls........................ 22

Peanut Banana Loaf............................ 22

Whole-Wheat Bagels........................... 22

Eggs in Tomato Sauce......................... 23

Baked Potato Skins............................ 23

Herbed Vegetable Breakfast.................... 24

Crustless Broccoli Quiche 24

Apple Chicken Sausage 24

Sirloin Steak and Eggs 25

Baked Hard Eggs.............................. 25

Flavourful Asparagus Strata................... 25

Prawn Frittata 26

Tasty Scotch Eggs 26

Omelet Cups................................. 26

Berry Muffins................................ 26

Cranberry Beignets........................... 27

Homemade Pancake 27

Chapter 2 Vegetable and Side Recipes..28

Breaded Avocado Fries......................... 28

Spicy Pickle Fries 28

Crisp Carrot Chips 28

Spicy Corn on Cob............................ 29

Bacon with Brussels Sprouts 29

Roasted Tomatoes............................. 29

Breaded Bell Pepper Strips 29

Roasted Broccoli 30

Flavourful Broccoli............................ 30

Delicious Broccoli Cheese Tots 30

Balsamic Asparagus........................... 31

Roasted Cauliflower 31

Spinach-Cheese–Stuffed Mushrooms....... 31

Breaded Green Beans 32

Simple Green Beans and Potatoes 32

Crunchy Potatoes 32

Delicious Sweet Potatoes 32

Cheese Portobello Pizzas 33

Homemade Veggie Burger 33

Garlic Asparagus 34

Easy Rainbow Carrots 34

Blistered Peppers 34

Buttered Green Beans with Almonds 34

Simple Fried Broccoli 35

Sesame Carrots 35

Honey Brussels Sprouts 35

Healthy Butternut Squash Purée 35

Simple Roasted Shallots 35

Cheese Courgette Fritters 36

Ears of Corn 36

Baked Sweet Potatoes with Brown Sugar. 36

Dijon Roasted Purple Potatoes 37

Cream Mashed Potatoes 37

Red Hassel-backs 37

Twice-Baked Potatoes 38

Chapter 3 Snack and Appetizer Recipes 39

Tasty Pot Stickers 39

Special Beef-Mango Skewers 39

Curried Sweet Potato Fries 39

Kale Chips with Yoghurt Sauce.............. 39

Artichoke Triangles 40

Delicious Spinach Dip with Bread Knots... 40

Homemade Arancini 41

Pesto Bruschetta................................ 41

Fried Tortellini with Mayonnaise 41

Breaded Shrimp Toast 41

Parmesan Hash Brown Bruschetta 42

Waffle Fry Poutine............................... 42

Buffalo Chicken Bites with Blue Cheese ... 42

Flavorful Chicken Wings 43

Easy Potato Chips 43

Panko Onion Rings 43

Bacon-Wrapped Jalapeño Poppers 44

Cream Cheese Wontons 44

Lime Tortilla Chips............................... 44

Corn Beef Hot Dogs 44

Butter Cheese Crackers........................ 45

Turkey Meatballs 45

Homemade Mozzarella Sticks 45

Lean Pork-Egg Rolls............................. 46

Beef Taco Meatballs 46

Parmesan Croutons 46

Russet Potato Skins 46

Hot Chicken Wings 47

Korean-Style Chicken Wings 47

Bread Crumbs Fried Pickles................... 47

Cinnamon Apple Chips 48

Broccoli Carrot Bites 48

Bacon-Wrapped Jalapeños 48

Cheese-Stuffed Mushrooms 49

Super Easy Pepperoni Chips.................. 49

Bacon-Wrapped Onion Slices 49

Chapter 4 Fish and Seafood Recipes 50

Lemony Shrimp 50

Cajun Salmon Fillets 50

Spiced Shrimp 50

Tasty Coconut Shrimps 50

Foil-Packet Lemon Salmon.................... 51

Fish Fingers...................................... 51

Crispy Salmon Patties 51

Crab Legs with Lemon Butter Dip 51

Delicious Firecracker Shrimp................. 52

Foil-Packet Lobster Tail with Parsley 52

Tuna Courgette Casserole.................... 52

Cream Prawn Scampi........................... 52

Fried Tuna Avocado Balls...................... 53

Fish Vegetable Bowl............................ 53

Spiced Crab Dip 53

Almond Salmon Fillets.......................... 54

Mayonnaise Crab Cakes 54

Coriander Baked Salmon 54

Sesame Tuna Steak............................. 54

Salmon Jerky 55

Prawn-Vegetable Kebabs..................... 55

Easy Buttery Cod 55

Lemon Crab-Stuffed Mushrooms 56

Tasty Steamer Clams 56

Butter Bay Scallops 56

Smoky Calamari Rings.......................... 56

Breaded Fish Sticks 57

Crab Cakes with Watercress Salad.......... 57

Bacon Stuffed Prawns........................... 58

Easy Raw Prawn 58

Lime–Crusted Halibut Fillets 58

Tuna Croquettes with Dill 58

Tuna on Tomatoes 59

Smoked Salmon with Baked Avocados 59

Salmon Cakes with Special Sauce 59

Lemon Jumbo Sea Scallops 60

Chapter 5 Poultry Recipes 61

Prep Day Chicken Breasts 61

Salsa Verde Chicken............................. 61

Chicken Bulgogi with Rice 61

Breaded Drumettes 61

Flavourful Chicken Legs 62

Greek Chicken Salad 62

Barbecue Chicken Legs 63

Cream Chicken Patties.......................... 63

Chicken Satay Kebabs 63

Curry Chicken Salad 64

Chicken Club Sandwiches...................... 64

Chicken Cobb Salad............................. 65

Delicious Chicken Avocado Paninis.......... 65

Breaded Chicken Strips......................... 65

Mustard Chicken Bites 66

Chicken Parmesan Pizzadillas................ 66

Lemony Chicken Meatballs 66

Jalapeño Chicken Meatballs 67

Chicken Quesadillas 67

Cheese Spaghetti Pie........................... 67

Buttermilk Cornish Hen 68

Savory Wings 68

Garlicky Wings.................................... 69

Fajita Chicken Thigh Meatballs 69

Pesto Chicken Pizzas........................... 69

Cheese Broccoli–Stuffed Chicken 69

Pickle-Brined Chicken 70

Spiced Chicken Thighs 70

Pork Rind Fried Chicken 70

Palatable Chipotle Drumsticks 71

Parmesan Drumsticks 71

Pecan-Crusted Chicken 71

Flavourful Chicken Tenders.................... 71

Bacon Chicken 72

Cheese Ham Chicken 72

Cheese Chicken Nuggets 72

Ginger Chicken Thigh Pieces 72

Chipotle Chicken Wings......................... 73

Cajun Chicken Bites............................. 73

Chapter 6 Beef, Pork, and Lamb Recipes 74

Blue Cheese Beef Burgers 74

Stuffed Bell Peppers 74

Mini Beef Meatloaves 74

Mushroom-Beef Balls 75

Steak-Veggie Kebabs............................ 75

Mushroom Steak Bites 75

Beef and Broccoli Bowls 76

BBQ Beef Bowls 76

Beef Chimichangas 77

Tasty Steak Fingers 77

Sirloin Steak Roll-Ups 77

Simple Rib Eye Steak............................ 78

Glazed Pork-Apple Skewers 78

Panko Breaded Pork Cutlets................... 78

Chili Pork Loin..................................... 79

Spiced Pork Chops............................... 79

Breaded Thin Pork Chops 79

Pork Meatball Bowl 79

Pineapple Pork Sliders 80

Pork and Salad 80

Coconut Pork Satay............................. 80

Pork Cabbage Burgers 81

Mustard Pork Tenderloin 81

Pork Tenderloin with Apple Slices 81

Grilled Pork Tenderloin 82

Pork Tenderloin with Potatoes............... 82

Pork-Fruit Kebabs 82

Steak-Vegetable Kebabs 82

Simple Grilled Steaks 83

Greek Vegetable Beef Bowl 83

Light Herbed Beef Meatballs 83

Beef-Stuffed Peppers........................... 84

Beef Broccoli in Stock 84

Stir-Fried Beef and Fruit 84

Parmesan Beef Risotto......................... 85

Butter Ribeye Steak 85

Garlicky Steak 85

Easy Filet Mignon 86

Worcestershire Short Ribs 86

Chapter 7 Dessert Recipes 87

Honey Pears with Ricotta 87

Grilled Fruit Skewers 87

Greek Peaches with Blueberries 87

Walnut-Stuffed Apples 87

Honey Apple-Peach Crisp 88

Strawberry Crumble 88

Berries Crumble.................................. 88

Apple-Blueberry Pies............................ 89

Oatmeal-Carrot Cups 89

Dark Chocolate Cookies......................... 89

Vanilla Lava Cakes 90

Cinnamon Pretzel Bites 90

Homemade Brownies 91

Chocolate Doughnut Holes..................... 91

Lemon Bars 91

Vanilla Chocolate Chip Cookies............... 92

Golden Peanut Butter Cookies 92

Snickerdoodles 92

Almond-Shortbread Cookies 92

Peach Oat Crumble.............................. 93

Simple Vanilla Cheesecake 93

Chocolate Cheesecake 93

Cheese Pound Cake 94

Cinnamon Apple Fritters....................... 94

Vanilla Pumpkin Pie 94

Peanut Cookies 95

Caramel Apples................................... 95

Mayonnaise Chocolate Cake................... 95

Easy-to-Make Coconut Cupcakes 96

Lemon Butter Cookies........................... 96

Cherry Pies.. 96

Chocolate Brownies 97

Giant Chocolate Cookies....................... 97

Conclusion 98

Appendix Recipes Index 99

Introduction

The Tower Air Fryer cooking appliance is an easy way to cook delicious and healthy meals. People are too busy in their life, and they have no time to cook food in their kitchen for long time. They also want to eat healthy and yummy food in significantly less time. The tower air fryer cooking appliance will take less time and prepare delicious food. When you have no time for cooking, this cooking appliance will become your perfect companion in your kitchen. This little machine can cook almost everything you put in it and yield amazing and tasty food prepared in less time with fewer calories.

However, if you are new to the air fryer world, you may be confused about how the tower air fryer works or face some difficulties while using it. The tower air fryer is easy to use if you know what you are doing. It has user-friendly operating buttons.

The best thing about this appliance is that it is enough for your big family because it has a large capacity to cook food for the whole family. You don't need to cook food in batches. It comes with a control panel that shows cooking time and temperature. It has useful accessories like an air fryer basket, cooking tray, and racks. With the tower air fryer cooking appliance, your food will be delicious, tender, juicy, and healthy and will cook in less time.

The best thing is that the cleaning method is simple. When the tower air fryer is cooled completely, wipe the inside and outside with a moist cloth. The accessories of the tower air fryer can go right into the dishwasher. It takes less time to clean than utensils. You can relax and enjoy yourself with your family instead of being tired in your kitchen. You didn't need to stand for a long time in your kitchen.

In my cookbook, I included tower air fryer recipes for you; you can cook them in this appliance quickly. You will learn how to use the tower air fryer in unique ways and get safety tips, prepare food in the air fryer, and figure out how to solve problems that may arise during cooking with your device.

Happy air frying!

What is Tower Air Fryer?

Tower has the most extensive range of air fryers in the UK and guarantees to meet all air frying needs. The benefit is that it comes with Vortex technology and cooks food 30% faster than other air fryers. It yields fat-free meals. The Tower air fryer cooks food by circulating hot air around the food through a traditional convection mechanism. It works like a convection oven. The hot air is created by a high-speed fan, which allows the cooking of crispy and tender food. The tower air fryer cooking appliance releases heat through a heating element which cooks delicious food. There is an exhaust fan right above the cooking chamber. It provides the same heating temperature for every single part of the food. The cleaning process is super easy. The operating buttons are user-friendly. The tower air fryer has no odor at all, and it is a safe cooking appliance. It is an environment-friendly cooking appliance. The internal pressure increases the temperature of the tower air fryer, which is controlled by the exhaust system. Use less oil for cooking while using this appliance. We recommended that to shake the air fryer basket while cooking food. Moreover, it saves energy and allows you to cook food within 15 minutes with different cooking options.

Benefits of Using Tower Air Fryer

Tower air fryer cooking appliance has many benefits to make your life easier. It is a household countertop device which utilizes high-speed fans to cook food delicious and crispy. There are a lot of benefits to using this advanced cooking appliance.

Large capacity:
The tower air fryer cooking appliance has a large capacity and is perfect for the whole family. You didn't need to prepare food in batches. You can prepare every type of food in the air fryer basket. Prepare the food for any festival.

Preserve the nutrients:
It will not lose nutrients and yield healthy and delicious meals. It preserves the essential nutrients in the food.

99% less fat:
It uses only minimal oil to make mealtime healthier, cooking all of your favorite fried food with 99% less fat. It makes your food delicious and tender. It saves your time and money also. Fat is not good for health. This appliance yields fat-free food. You can eat fried food without any trouble.

Low energy consumption:
It cooks food 30% faster. Tower air fryer cooking appliance uses less energy than conventional ovens. It saves up to 50% energy by switching to air fryer cooking.

Safe and fast cooking appliance:
The tower air fryer cooking appliance is a trouble-safe appliance. It works faster than other air fryers. You didn't need to spend a lot of time in the kitchen. Your food will be ready in significantly less time, you can create crispy and delicious meals within 15minutes by using a tower air fryer appliance. The towel air fryer does not produce too much heat and steam, and it does not heat the environment. It is environment-friendly appliance. There is no risk of spilling or splashing oil like traditional deep fryers. It avoids burning the food.

Provide healthy food:
The towel air fryer provides healthy food. The best thing about this appliance is that it takes less fat or oil to prepare food. It is good choice for your diet. You can cook whatever you want. It will not affect your health.

No stove or oven needed:
The towel air fryer cooking appliance has so many cooking functions. You didn't need to use a stove or oven. It is the best appliance for busy weekend nights. It does not provide steam.

Super easy cleaning method:
This appliance is super easy to clean. Don't put the appliance in the dishwasher. It will damage your appliance. The air fryer has removable parts. Before cleaning, it allows you to remove the parts. Many of these parts are dishwasher-safe. The cleaning method is super easy. The main unit is not dishwasher-safe. Wipe it with a damp cloth. Before cleaning, unplug the air fryer from the outlet. I added all details of cleaning the appliance in the cookbook. Please read it briefly.

Versatile and prepare all types of meals:
It is a versatile appliance and prepares any meals. You can prepare all types of food in the appliance. For example, chicken, beef, lamb, veggies, desserts, and many more.

Vortex technology:
The tower air fryer comes with Vortex technology and cooks food 30% faster than other air fryers.

Minimal mess:
Using towel air fryer cooking appliance, your whole kitchen will be clean – no splattering oil or multiple dirty pans or skillets. Plus, the air fryer basket is simple to clean – mostly non-stick and dishwasher-safe.

Adjustable temperature and timer:
This appliance has adjustable temperature control from 80 degrees Fahrenheit to 200 degrees Fahrenheit. It has a 1-hour timer with an automatic shut-off feature for accurate cooking.

Good companion for busy moms:
The towel air fryer is a good companion in your kitchen. Prepare the ingredients and add them to the air fryer basket. Adjust the cooking time, temperature, and desired cooking functions and start cooking.

Before First Use

Firstly, remove all packaging from the appliance. Make sure that there is no packet remaining in the appliance. After that, check your appliance to ensure there is no damage to the cord or any visible damage to the appliance. Then, dispose of the package. Remove any label from the appliance. Clean the towel air fryer with warm water, a non-abrasive sponge, or washing-up liquid. Then, wipe the outside and inside of the unit with a damp or moist cloth. Don't overfill the air fryer with oil or fat. It needs very little to no oil and operates using hot air.

Operating Buttons of the Towel Air Fryer

There are so many options on the control panel.

There are the followings:

Auto-cooking program – fries: You can prepare fried food using this cooking function. Examples include French fries, Chicken nuggets, Crispy cheese rolls, Fried chicken, Fried rice, and many more.

Auto-cooking program – steak: You can prepare any steak using this cooking function. For example, beef steaks, veggie steaks, chicken steaks, etc.

Auto-cooking program – drumsticks: Prepare chicken drumsticks using this cooking function.

Auto-cooking program – fish: You can prepare crab, scallops, fish, and many more fish recipes using this cooking function.

Auto-cooking program – shrimp: This function is used for making shrimp recipes. Prepare shrimp fajita, shrimp salad, and many more.

Auto-cooking program – roast chicken: It is used to roast the chicken. Press this button if you want to cook roasted chicken.

Auto-cooking program – Rotisserie

Auto-cooking program - dried fruit: This cooking program is used to dry the fruits.

Fan indicator

Heating indicator

Temperature indicator: This operating button shows the temperature of the food.

Timer indicator: This operating button shows the timer while cooking food.

Temperature up key: You can use this operating key to increase the temperature according to the recipe instructions.

Temperature down key: You can use this operating key to decrease the temperature according to the recipe instructions.

Light ON/OFF key: You can turn on or off the light on the inner side of the unit.

Mode key

LCD screen: This LCD screen shows the temperature and timer while cooking food.

ON/Pause key: You can use this key to on/pause the cooking function.

Rotating rotisserie key

Timer up button: You can use this operating button to increase the time according to the recipe instructions.

Timer down button: You can use this operating button to decrease the time according to the recipe instructions.

Using the Appliance:
Using the towel air fryer is super easy. After reading the instructions, you will know how to use this appliance. Let's dig in!

Remove the door:
The towel air fryer has a removable door. You can easily remove it from the appliance and clean it. But, the question is "how to pull apart the door from the appliance." I will let you know the answer to your question. Firstly, push the door as far as it will go, approximately 70 degrees. Then, push the grooved latch horizontally on the right-hand side of the hinge to release the door. When the door has been released, pull it down to separate it from the appliance. If you want to reinstall the door, align the edges of the door with the holes on either side of the hinge and then insert it into the body of the unit.

Automatic switch off:
The tower air fryer has a timer that automatically shuts off the unit when the timer reaches zero. When you press the key, it will manually turn off the air fryer.

Preparing for use:
Put the appliance on a stable and horizontal, and even surface. Remember; don't put the unit onto the heating element. Pull the cord from the storage compartment, which is present at the end of the unit. Moreover, don't fill the air fryer with oil or other liquid. Don't put anything like a heavy skillet over the appliance. It will damage your appliance.

Tips for using accessories:
These are essential parts and accessories of this appliance. For cooking food, you need to use these accessories. These are the followings:
Control panel
Housing
Rotating cage
Slag tray
Door
Air outlet openings
Power cord
Air flow racks
BBQ skewers
Grilled chicken rack
Fetch the fork

Rotating Cage:
The rotating cage is perfect for French fries, roasted nuts, and other appetizers. You can use the fetch fork tool to put the basket into the unit.

Slag Tray:
The slag tray is easy to clean up. That's why; you can use it for cooking food.

Door:
The door is removable and super easy to install and uninstall. I added the details to remove and install the door.

Air Flow Racks:
You can use these racks for dehydrating food and cooking crispy snacks or reheating items such as pizza and frittata.

BBQ Skewers:
The BBQ skewer is perfect for kebab recipes. Such as veggies, fish, chicken, and beef recipes! Thread the meat onto the BBQ skewers and put it into the air fryer basket.

Grilled Chicken Racks:
It is used for roasts and whole chicken. Ensure the chicken is not too large to rotate freely within the air fryer basket. It should be 1.5 kg.

Fetch the fork:
You can use this fork to remove the cooked and roasted chicken. You can add food into the air fryer basket using fetch a fork.

Step-By-Step Air Frying

Using the towel air fryer is super simple. I will guide you on how to cook food in the towel air fryer cooking appliance. If you follow these instructions, you can easily prepare food for yourself and your family. Here is step-by-step guidance on using a towel air fryer and cooking delicious food. Follow these simple instructions:

If you have a new air fryer, clean it firstly:
For initial use, you should clean the air fryer thoroughly. Remove the packaging and accessories from the air fryer cooking appliance. Place the air fryer basket and reversible tray into the dishwasher and clean it with warm soapy water. Remove any dust with a clean and soft cloth. Remove the main unit with a damp cloth. When all air fryer parts get dry, return to the main unit.

Select a recipe and read it:
I added your favorite towel air fryer recipes to the cookbook. You can choose the desired recipe from the book and read it two times.

Purchase the fresh ingredients:
If you want good results, buy fresh ingredients and spices for good health. You should choose fresh ingredients for your good diet.

Prepare the food:
Before cooking, prepare all ingredients and measure them according to the recipe instructions. Place the vegetables onto the cutting board and cut in the same size to cook evenly. If you want to marinate the meat, then plan. If you are using frozen food, allow it to thaw if needed. Rinse the vegetables or fruits under running water and remove excess liquid.

Spray the food with non-stick cooking spray:
Purchase high-quality cooking spray and spray it with non-stick cooking spray before seasoning the food. It is important because seasoning will stick to the food, and the appliance will not produce white smoke. Spray the chicken, seafood fillets, and vegetable pieces before placing them into the air fryer basket.

Air frying:

Connect the main plugs to the wall outlet. Open the tower air fryer door. Add ingredients into the air fryer basket using fetch the fork. Close the air fryer door. The air fryer appliance beeping sound and all the indicators will light up momentarily. After a few seconds, all of the indicators will go off except for the on/pause key indicator, which will remain illuminated to indicate the appliance is turned on but in standby mode.

You can press this key while the unit is in this mode to bring up the touch control panel. But, if you don't press the key after the control panel is lit, the tower air fryer will automatically go into standby mode after 90 seconds.

Use the temperature up or down key; select the desired temperature according to the recipe instructions. Use the time up or down key; select the desired cooking time according to the recipe instructions. The time will increase or decrease in the increment of 1 minute from 0 up to 60 minutes. The temperature will increase or decrease in increments of 5 degrees, from 30 up to 200 degrees.

Note: The cooking time and temperature can be changed or adjusted at any time while the air fryer is in operation.

Cooking Tips

Cooking food is super simple and cooking is an art. If you are a newbie in cooking, you should follow these steps:

• Clean the utensils, bowls, and pantry items before cooking. Clean the work surface and cutting board. Rinse the veggies and meat under clean water.

• Wear a comfortable dress while cooking, and you won't have to worry about getting dirty.

• Measure your ingredients according to the recipe instructions. Place ingredients separately in the small bowls.

• Always read your recipe two times before cooking.

• If you were using butter into the pan and worried about over-browning, then use a little bit of lemon juice.

- Cook with kosher salt and sprinkle with sea salt because it is the best choice.
- If you didn't find shallot, then use onion and garlic instead of shallot.
- Break the egg on a paper towel onto the counter because it is easy to clean.
- Always taste your food before seasoning, or it will spoil your food.
- Don't rinse pasta.
- Remove the thick and rough stems of leafy green with your hands.
- Keep your spices and herbs away from the heat source because it loses their flavor.
- Store fresh herbs into the glass of water and place it into the fridge.
- To prevent tears, cut off the root of the onion before slicing.
- You can use an egg slicer to cut small fruits such as kiwis.
- Keep knives sharp before using.
- Freeze leftover tomato paste into the ice cubes containers.
- Cut butter into pieces and melt it for 10 to 15 minutes at room temperature to soften the butter.
- If you want to grate the soft cheese, place it into the fridge for 30 minutes.
- Save money by purchasing seasoned fresh vegetables and fruits and then freeze them into the air-tight container.
- Always taste your dish before serving.
- Always put the blender onto the countertop.

Straight from the Store

If you want to store the appliance, put it into the packaging after deep cleaning. Make sure that all parts are clean and dry. Put it into the dark and cool area. Store it on a flat and dry surface out of reach of children. Make sure that, the appliance is cool. Door is fully shut down.

Cleaning and Caring of Tower Air Fryer

The cleaning procedure of the tower air fryer is super simple. There are some rules you should follow to maintain the air fryer:

- Utensils such as steel wire brushes, metal utensils, and abrasive sponges can damage the surface of the appliance. Don't use it to remove the leftover food from the air fryer basket. It can damage the surface of the basket. You can use degreasing liquid to remove any remaining dirt.
- Don't immerse the main unit into the dishwasher. Otherwise, it will damage your appliance.
- Before cleaning, unplug the main unit from the outlet. Don't immerse the outlet into the water.
- Clean the air fryer after every use. All parts of the air fryer are removable. Before cleaning, allow the main unit to cool. Remove the accessories from the main unit. Use oven mitts or tongs to remove the parts because they can be hot.
- Use the damp cloth or non-abrasive sponge for cleaning the interior or outer side of the main unit.
- To remove the grease from the air fryer basket, soak it overnight into warm and soapy water. The next day, it will remove easily.
- Use a soft scrub brush, dish soap, baking soda, and a clean cloth for deep cleaning. The process of deep cleaning is that:
- Unplug the appliance and allow it to cool for 30 minutes. Remove the pan and basket from the air fryer and wash them with hot water and soap. If you see grease on these parts, soak them in hot water for 10 minutes. Then, scrub with a non-abrasive sponge.
- Clean the interior of the basket with dish soap and wipe it with a damp cloth. Remove the door of the main unit and rinse it under clean water.
- Wipe the appliance with a moist or damp cloth carefully.
- If you see stubborn residue onto the basket, make the mixture of baking soda and water and scrub it into the grim with a soft brush.
- When all parts get dry, return to the main unit.
- To avoid any smell or odor, clean the ring after every use.
- You can assemble it again. Return all accessories to the appliance.

Helpful tips:

- For best results, remove the food immediately after cooking to avoid burning.
- Place the food into the air fryer basket in one layer to get tender and browning food.
- Don't touch the surface of the main unit while cooking food. Use oven mitts or tongs.
- Adjust the desired temperature and cooking time onto the display screen.
- When you open the lid during food, the cooking time will pause. When you close the top, the cooking time will resume.
- Avoid overcooking.
- Use 1 tbsp of oil for cooking vegetables. It takes little to no oil for cooking food.
- Don't immerse the main unit into the water.
- Don't overfill the basket with any other liquid.
- Clean the appliance after every use.
- Check the voltage of the main circuit before operating the appliance.
- Turn off at the wall socket then remove the plug from the socket when not in use or before cleaning the appliance.
- Don't permission your children to play with appliance.
- Don't use any extension cord with this appliance.
- Don't pull the plug out by the cord otherwise your appliance will damage.

Troubleshooting

Problem 1: The tower air fryer is not working

Possible reason: The appliance is not completely plugged in. You have not adjusted the time.

Solution: Again plug in into the wall outlet. Adjust the time again.

Problem 2: The food is not fried well.

Possible reason: The amount of ingredients is large. You adjust the temperature and time is too low for this.

Solution: If the amount of ingredients is very large, cook the food in batches. Smaller batches are fried more evenly. Again adjust the temperature and time while cooking food.

Type of Food with Temperature

Fish:
Medium to well done: 130°F to 150°F
Chicken/turkey:
Well done: 165°F
Pork:
Medium to well done: 130°F to 160°F
Beef/lamb:
Rare: 115°F
Medium rare: 125°F
Medium to well done: 130°F to 150°F

Wiring Safety for UK Use Only

The wires are label in following:
Blue neutral [N] Brown live [L] Green or Yellow [Earth]
The wire label **brown** is live wire and must be connected with terminal marked **[L]**.
The wire label **green or yellow** must be connected with terminal marked **[E]**.
The wire label **blue** is a neutral and must be connected to terminal marked **[N]**.

4-Week Diet Plan

Week 1

Day 1:
Breakfast: Cinnamon Bagels
Lunch: Crisp Carrot Chips
Snack: Fried Tortellini with Mayonnaise
Dinner: Delicious Firecracker Shrimp
Dessert: Homemade Brownies

Day 2:
Breakfast: Hash Browns
Lunch: Roasted Tomatoes
Snack: Waffle Fry Poutine
Dinner: Stuffed Bell Peppers
Dessert: Lemon Bars

Day 3:
Breakfast: Baked Peaches Oatmeal
Lunch: Flavourful Broccoli
Snack: Panko Onion Rings
Dinner: Mustard Chicken Bites
Dessert: Peach Oat Crumble

Day 4:
Breakfast: Whole-Wheat Bagels
Lunch: Delicious Sweet Potatoes
Snack: Lime Tortilla Chips
Dinner: Coriander Baked Salmon
Dessert: Chocolate Cheesecake

Day 5:
Breakfast: Baked Potato Skins
Lunch: Garlic Asparagus
Snack: Butter Cheese Crackers
Dinner: Simple Rib Eye Steak
Dessert: Honey Apple-Peach Crisp

Day 6:
Breakfast: Crustless Broccoli Quiche
Lunch: Sesame Carrots
Snack: Lean Pork-Egg Rolls
Dinner: Chicken Club Sandwiches
Dessert: Vanilla Pumpkin Pie

Day 7:
Breakfast: Sirloin Steak and Eggs
Lunch: Blistered Peppers
Snack: Parmesan Croutons
Dinner: Easy Buttery Cod
Dessert: Caramel Apples

Week 2

Day 1:
Breakfast: Flavourful Asparagus Strata
Lunch: Roasted Cauliflower
Snack: Korean-Style Chicken Wings
Dinner: Mushroom Steak Bites
Dessert: Strawberry Crumble

Day 2:
Breakfast: Eggs in Tomato Sauce
Lunch: Breaded Green Beans
Snack: Turkey Meatballs
Dinner: Breaded Drumettes
Dessert: Oatmeal-Carrot Cups

Day 3:
Breakfast: Banana-Nut Muffins
Lunch: Roasted Broccoli
Snack: Curried Sweet Potato Fries
Dinner: Foil-Packet Lemon Salmon
Dessert: Greek Peaches with Blueberries

Day 4:
Breakfast: Toaster Pastries
Lunch: Spicy Corn on Cob
Snack: Artichoke Triangles
Dinner: Pork Cabbage Burgers
Dessert: Grilled Fruit Skewers

Day 5:
Breakfast: Easy Jam Doughnuts
Lunch: Bacon with Brussels Sprouts
Snack: Kale Chips with Yoghurt Sauce
Dinner: Steak-Vegetable Kebabs
Dessert: Vanilla Lava Cakes

Day 6:
Breakfast: Cinnamon Doughnut Holes
Lunch: Breaded Bell Pepper Strips
Snack: Tasty Pot Stickers
Dinner: Chicken Quesadillas
Dessert: Simple Vanilla Cheesecake

Day 7:
Breakfast: Raisin Granola Bars
Lunch: Healthy Butternut Squash Purée
Snack: Homemade Arancini
Dinner: Smoky Calamari Rings
Dessert: Snickerdoodles

Week 3

Day 1:
Breakfast: Oat Blueberry Muffins
Lunch: Easy Rainbow Carrots
Snack: Broccoli Carrot Bites
Dinner: Chili Pork Loin
Dessert: Cinnamon Apple Fritters

Day 2:
Breakfast: Pepper & Onion Hash
Lunch: Balsamic Asparagus
Snack: Flavorful Chicken Wings
Dinner: Tasty Steamer Clams
Dessert: Vanilla Chocolate Chip Cookies

Day 3:
Breakfast: Tasty Scotch Eggs
Lunch: Cheese Courgette Fritters
Snack: Cheese-Stuffed Mushrooms
Dinner: Garlicky Wings
Dessert: Dark Chocolate Cookies

Day 4:
Breakfast: Cranberry Beignets
Lunch: Simple Fried Broccoli
Snack: Bacon-Wrapped Onion Slices
Dinner: Spiced Chicken Thighs
Dessert: Apple-Blueberry Pies

Day 5:
Breakfast: Hard Boiled Eggs
Lunch: Dijon Roasted Purple Potatoes
Snack: Beef Taco Meatballs
Dinner: Grilled Pork Tenderloin
Dessert: Honey Pears with Ricotta

Day 6:
Breakfast: Puffed Egg Tarts
Lunch: Red Hassel-backs
Snack: Hot Chicken Wings
Dinner: Fish Vegetable Bowl
Dessert: Almond-Shortbread Cookies

Day 7:
Breakfast: Scrambled Eggs
Lunch: Simple Roasted Shallots
Snack: Easy Potato Chips
Dinner: Pork Meatball Bowl
Dessert: Lemon Butter Cookies

Week 4

Day 1:
Breakfast: Toast Sticks
Lunch: Cheese Portobello Pizzas
Snack: Breaded Shrimp Toast
Dinner: Lemony Chicken Meatballs
Dessert: Cinnamon Pretzel Bites

Day 2:
Breakfast: Granola Cereal
Lunch: Honey Brussels Sprouts
Snack: Cream Cheese Wontons
Dinner: BBQ Beef Bowls
Dessert: Berries Crumble

Day 3:
Breakfast: Peanut Banana Loaf
Lunch: Simple Green Beans and Potatoes
Snack: Pesto Bruschetta
Dinner: Crispy Salmon Patties
Dessert: Golden Peanut Butter Cookies

Day 4:
Breakfast: Apple Chicken Sausage
Lunch: Delicious Broccoli Cheese Tots
Snack: Corn Beef Hot Dogs
Dinner: Tasty Steak Fingers
Dessert: Chocolate Doughnut Holes

Day 5:
Breakfast: Baked Hard Eggs
Lunch: Spinach-Cheese–Stuffed Mushrooms
Snack: Russet Potato Skins
Dinner: Chicken Cobb Salad
Dessert: Cherry Pies

Day 6:
Breakfast: Prawn Frittata
Lunch: Crunchy Potatoes
Snack: Cinnamon Apple Chips
Dinner: Bacon Stuffed Prawns
Dessert: Chocolate Brownies

Day 7:
Breakfast: Omelet Cups
Lunch: Homemade Veggie Burger
Snack: Bacon-Wrapped Jalapeños
Dinner: Mushroom-Beef Balls
Dessert: Peanut Cookies

Cinnamon Doughnut Holes

Prep Time: 5 minutes | **Cook Time:** 5 minutes | **Serves:** 4

Oil, for spraying
1 (340g) can of refrigerated buttermilk biscuits
50g of sugar1 tablespoon of ground cinnamon

1. Preheat the air fryer to 175°C. 2. Line the air fryer basket with baking paper, and lightly spray it with oil. 3. Cut each biscuit into 4 pieces, and then roll each piece into balls. 4. Place the balls in the air fryer basket and lightly spray with oil. You can work in batches. 5. Cook the balls in the preheated air fryer for 5 minutes until browned. 6. Mix the sugar and cinnamon in a bag. 7. Lightly spray the doughnut holes with oil, and immediately transfer them to the bag; close the bag and shake well to coat the doughnut holes with the mixture. 8. Transfer the doughnut holes to the serving plate and enjoy.

Per Serving: Calories 320; Fat 11.27g; Sodium 853mg; Carbs 49.52g; Fibre 3.4g; Sugar 13.12g; Protein 5.85g

Easy Jam Doughnuts

Prep Time: 10 minutes | **Cook Time:** 5 minutes | **Serves:** 8

Oil, for spraying
1 (450g) can of refrigerated large biscuits
100g of sugar
8 tablespoons of jam of choice
5 tablespoons of unsalted butter, melted

1. Preheat the air fryer to 180°C. 2. Line the air fryer basket with baking and spray lightly with oil. 3. Separate each biscuit into eight pieces. Place the dough in the prepared basket. 4. Cook the dough in the preheated air fryer for 5 minutes until browned. 5. Place the sugar in a shallow bowl and spoon the jam into a pastry bag. 6. Brush the doughnuts with the melted butter, and immediately dredge in the sugar, then transfer to a plate to cool for a while. 7. Poke a hole in the sides of each doughnut, and then carefully pipe the jam from the bag into the hole of each doughnut. 8. Enjoy.

Per Serving: Calories 309; Fat 12.78g; Sodium 538mg; Carbs 45.54g; Fibre 0.9g; Sugar 16.69g; Protein 3.86g

Toast Sticks

Prep Time: 10 minutes | **Cook Time:** 9 minutes | **Serves:** 4

Oil, for spraying
6 large eggs
355ml of milk
2 teaspoons of vanilla extract
1 teaspoon of ground cinnamon
8 slices of bread, cut into thirds
Syrup of choice, for serving

1. Preheat the air fryer to 185°C. Line the air fryer basket with baking paper and spray with oil. 2. Whisk the eggs, milk, vanilla, and cinnamon in a small bowl. 3. Dunk one piece of bread in the egg mixture, making sure to coat both sides (work quickly so the bread doesn't get soggy) and then immediately transfer the bread to the air fryer basket. 4. Do the same with the remaining bread, and make sure the pieces don't touch each other. You can work in batches. 5. Cook the bread pieces in the preheated air fryer for 9 minutes, flipping halfway through. 6. When cooked, enjoy the bread slices with your favourite syrup.

Per Serving: Calories 271; Fat 11.13g; Sodium 338mg; Carbs 24.98g; Fibre 1.4g; Sugar 6.92g; Protein 15.54g

Toaster Pastries

Prep Time: 10 minutes | **Cook Time:** 11 minutes | **Serves:** 6

Oil, for spraying
1 (425g) packet of refrigerated piecrust
6 tablespoons of jam or preserve of choice
240g of icing sugar
3 tablespoons of milk
1 to 2 tablespoons of sprinkles of choice

1. Preheat the air fryer to 175°C. Line the air fryer basket with baking and spray lightly with oil. 2. Cut the piecrust into 12 rectangles, about 75 by 100mm each. You will need to re-roll the dough scraps to get 12 rectangles. 3. Spread 1 tablespoon of jam in the centre of 6 rectangles, leaving 6mm around the edges. 4. Pour some water into a small bowl and use the water to moisten the edge of each rectangle. 5. Top each rectangle with another and use your fingers to press around the edges. Using the tines of a fork, seal the edges of the dough and poke a few holes in the top of each one. Place the pastries in the prepared basket. 6. Cook the pastries for 11 minutes. Let them cool completely after cooking. 7. Mix the icing sugar and milk in a medium bowl. Spread the icing over the tops of the pastries and add sprinkles. 8. Serve immediately.
Per Serving: Calories 513; Fat 20.1g; Sodium 212mg; Carbs 84.14g; Fibre 7.2g; Sugar 68.73g; Protein 2.53g

Granola Cereal

Prep Time: 10 minutes | **Cook Time:** 30 minutes | **Serves:** 7

Oil, for spraying
135g of gluten-free rolled oats
75g of chopped walnuts
75g of chopped almonds
60g pumpkin seeds
60g of maple syrup or honey
1 tablespoon of toasted sesame oil or vegetable oil
1 teaspoon of ground cinnamon
½ teaspoon salt
65g dried cranberries

1. Preheat the air fryer to 120°C. Line the air fryer basket with baking and spray lightly with oil. 2. Combine the oats, walnuts, almonds, pumpkin seeds, maple syrup, sesame oil, cinnamon, and salt in a large bowl. 3. Arrange the mixture in an even layer in the prepared basket. 4. Cook the mixture in the preheated air fryer for 30 minutes, stirring every 10 minutes. 5. Put the granola in a bowl, add the dried cranberries and toss to combine. 6. Let the dish cool to room temperature before storing in an airtight container.
Per Serving: Calories 182; Fat 9.9g; Sodium 191mg; Carbs 25.97g; Fibre 4.4g; Sugar 9.52g; Protein 7.1g

Raisin Granola Bars

Prep Time: 5 minutes | **Cook Time:** 15 minutes | **Serves:** 6

Oil, for spraying
110g of gluten-free rolled oats, divided
170g packed light brown sugar
1 teaspoon of ground cinnamon
115g of unsalted butter, melted
3 tablespoons of honey
1 tablespoon of vegetable oil
1 teaspoon of vanilla extract
2 tablespoons of raisins

1. Line the baking pan with baking paper and spray lightly with oil. 2. Pulse about half of the oats in a blender until smooth, and then transfer to a medium bowl. 3. Add the remaining oats, brown sugar, and cinnamon and stir to combine, then add the butter, honey, vegetable oil, and vanilla and stir to combine. Fold in the raisins. 4. Transfer the mixture to the baking pan and press into an even layer. 5. Cook the mixture at 160°C for 10 minutes. When the time is up, increase the heat to 180°C and cook for a further 5 minutes. 6. When cooked, let the dish cool to room temperature, and then freeze before cutting into bars and serving.
Per Serving: Calories 202; Fat 14.15g; Sodium 11mg; Carbs 22.8g; Fibre 3.3g; Sugar 9.29g; Protein 4.17g

Cinnamon Bagels

Prep Time: 30 minutes | **Cook Time:** 10 minutes | **Serves:** 4

Oil, for spraying
35g of raisins
125g of self-rising flour, plus more for dusting
280g of plain Greek yoghurt
1 teaspoon of ground cinnamon
1 large egg

1. Line the air fryer basket with baking and spray lightly with oil. 2. Place the raisins in a bowl of hot water and let them sit for 10 to 15 minutes until they have plumped. This will make them extra juicy. 3. In a large bowl, mix the flour, yoghurt, and cinnamon in a large bowl until a ball is formed. 4. Drain the raisins and gently work them into the ball of dough. 5. sprinkle flour onto the work surface and place the dough on it. Roll each piece into a 200 - or 230mm-long rope and shape it into a circle, pinching the ends together to seal. 6. Beat the egg in a bowl and brush the egg onto the top of the dough. 7. Place the dough in the prepared basket. 8. Cook the dough at 175°C for 10 minutes. 9. Serve warm.

Per Serving: Calories 163; Fat 3.43g; Sodium 403mg; Carbs 26.74g; Fibre 1.2g; Sugar 2.98g; Protein 5.92g

Banana-Nut Muffins

Prep Time: 5 minutes | **Cook Time:** 15 minutes | **Serves:** 10

Oil, for spraying
2 very ripe bananas
85g of packed light brown sugar
80g of canola oil or vegetable oil
1 large egg
1 teaspoon of vanilla extract
95g of all-purpose flour
1 teaspoon of baking powder
1 teaspoon of ground cinnamon
75g of chopped walnuts

1. Preheat the air fryer to 160°C. Spray 10 silicone muffin cups lightly with oil. 2. In a medium bowl, mash the bananas. 3. Add the brown sugar, canola oil, egg, and vanilla to the banana bowl, and stir to combine; fold in the flour, baking powder, and cinnamon; add the walnuts and fold a few times to distribute throughout the batter. 5. Divide the batter equally among the prepared muffin cups and place them in the basket. You can work in batches. 6. Cook the muffins in the preheated air fryer for 15 minutes, or until golden brown and a toothpick inserted into the centre of a muffin comes out clean. 7. Let the muffins cool on a wire rack before serving.

Per Serving: Calories 164; Fat 11.77g; Sodium 5mg; Carbs 13.36g; Fibre 1.2g; Sugar 2.76g; Protein 2.2g

Scrambled Eggs

Prep Time: 5 minutes | **Cook Time:** 10 minutes | **Serves:** 2

1 teaspoon of unsalted butter
2 large eggs
2 tablespoons of milk
2 tablespoons of shredded cheddar cheese
Salt
Freshly ground black pepper

1. Place the butter in the baking pan and cook in the air fryer at 150°C for 1 to 2 minutes until melted. 2. In a small bowl, beat the eggs with the milk and cheese and season with salt and black pepper. Transfer the mixture to the baking pan. 3. Cook for 3 minutes. Stir the eggs and push them toward the centre of the pan. 4. Cook for another 2 minutes, then stir again. 5. Cook for another 2 minutes, until the eggs are just cooked. 6. Serve warm.

Per Serving: Calories 88; Fat 6.93g; Sodium 171mg; Carbs 2.12g; Fibre 0g; Sugar 1.35g; Protein 4.2g

Hard Boiled Eggs

Prep Time: 5 minutes | **Cook Time:** 15 minutes | **Serves:** 6

Oil, for spraying
6 large eggs

1. Preheat the air fryer to 130°C. 2. Line the air fryer basket with baking and spray lightly

with oil. 2. Place the eggs in the air fryer basket. 3. Cook the eggs for 15 minutes. 4. Fill a bowl with water and ice, and then transfer the cooked eggs to the bowl; let the eggs sit for 1 minute or until cool enough to handle. 5. Use the paper towel to pat the eggs dry and serve immediately. 6. You can refrigerate the cooked eggs for up to 7 days.
Per Serving: Calories 72; Fat 4.76g; Sodium 71mg; Carbs 0.36g; Fibre 0g; Sugar 0.19g; Protein 6.28g

Puffed Egg Tarts

Prep Time: 10 minutes | **Cook Time:** 42 minutes | **Serves:** 4

Oil, for spraying
Plain flour, for dusting
1 (300g) sheet frozen puff pastry, thawed
100g shredded cheddar cheese, divided
4 large eggs
2 teaspoons chopped fresh parsley
Salt
Freshly ground black pepper

1. Preheat the air fryer to 200°C. Line the air fryer basket with parchment and spray lightly with oil. 2. Lightly dust the work surface with flour. Unfold the puff pastry and cut it into 4 equal squares. 3. Place 2 squares in the prepared basket. 4. Cook the tarts in the preheated air fryer for 10 minutes. 5. After cooking, take out the tarts and use spoon to press the centre to make an indentation. 5. Sprinkle 3 tablespoons of cheese into each indentation and crack 1 egg into the centre of each tart shell. 6. Cook for another 7 to 11 minutes, or until the eggs are cooked to your desired doneness. 7. Repeat with the remaining puff pastry squares, cheese, and eggs. 8. Sprinkle evenly with the parsley, and season with salt and black pepper. Serve immediately.
Per Serving: Calories 196; Fat 14.32g; Sodium 311mg; Carbs 10.08g; Fibre 0.4g; Sugar 1.7g; Protein 6.69g

Hash Browns

Prep Time: 30 minutes | **Cook Time:** 20 minutes | **Serves:** 4

Oil, for spraying
3 potatoes
2 tablespoons minced onion
1 teaspoon granulated garlic
½ teaspoon salt
¼ teaspoon freshly ground black pepper
2 teaspoons olive oil

1. Line the air fryer basket with parchment and spray lightly with oil. 2. Peel the potatoes and grate them against the largest holes on a box grater. 3. Prepare a bowl of cold water, and soak the potatoes in it for 20 minutes (this step will remove some of the starch and give you crunchier results). 4. Drain the potatoes, place them on several sheets of paper towels, roll them up, and squeeze out as much water as possible. 5. Transfer the potatoes to a large bowl, and mix them with the onion, garlic, salt, black pepper, and olive oil. 6. Spread the potato mixture in an even layer in the prepared air fryer basket, and cook them at 200°C for 10 minutes, shake, and cook for another 10 minutes, until browned and crispy. 7.Let the dish cool for 2 to 4 minutes before serving.
Per Serving: Calories 242; Fat 2.49g; Sodium 305mg; Carbs 50.82g; Fibre 3.7g; Sugar 1.94g; Protein 6.04g

Pepper & Onion Hash

Prep Time: 10 minutes | **Cook Time:** 30 minutes | **Serves:** 6

Oil, for spraying
3 medium potatoes, diced
½ yellow onion, diced
1 green pepper, seeded and diced
2 tablespoons olive oil
2 teaspoons granulated garlic
1 teaspoon salt
½ teaspoon freshly ground black pepper

1. Line the air fryer basket with parchment and spray lightly with oil. 2. Add the potatoes, onion, pepper, and olive oil to a large bowl, and then mix them with the garlic, salt, and black pepper. 3. Transfer the coated vegetables to the air fryer basket, and cook them at 200°C for 20 to 30 minutes until browned,

stirring them every 10 minutes to cook evenly. 4. Serve warm.

Per Serving: Calories 199; Fat 4.7g; Sodium 400mg; Carbs 36.6g; Fibre 2.8g; Sugar 2.92g; Protein 4.4g

Quiche

Prep Time: 10 minutes | **Cook Time:** 20 minutes | **Serves:** 6

Oil, for spraying
6 large eggs
120ml milk
170g sour cream
15g chopped baby spinach
70g diced ham
1 tablespoon minced onion
50g diced tomato
2 tablespoons bacon bits
1 tablespoon chopped fresh chives
100g shredded cheddar cheese, divided
1 (23cm) frozen piecrust, thawed

1. Line the air fryer basket with parchment and spray lightly with oil. 2. Mix the eggs, milk, sour cream, spinach, ham, onion, tomato, bacon bits, and chives in a bowl. 3. Sprinkle half of the cheese in the bottom of the piecrust, and pour the egg mixture over the cheese. 4. Place the quiche in the prepared basket, and cook at 150°C for 12 minutes. 5. When the time is up, top the quiche with the remaining cheese, and cook for 7 minutes more until the centre is set and the top is golden brown. 6. Let the quiche rest for 5 minutes before cutting into slices and serving.

Per Serving: Calories 241; Fat 17.48g; Sodium 305mg; Carbs 6.29g; Fibre 0.8g; Sugar 1.65g; Protein 14.42g

Oat Blueberry Muffins

Prep Time: 10 minutes | **Cook Time:** 15 minutes | **Serves:** 12

180g whole-wheat flour
60g oats
95g sugar
1 tablespoon baking powder
1 teaspoon ground cinnamon
½ teaspoon salt

240ml unsweetened vanilla almond milk
4 tablespoons unsalted butter, melted and cooled
2 eggs
1 teaspoon vanilla extract
150g organic blueberries

1. Combine the flour, oats, sugar, baking powder, cinnamon, and salt in a large bowl; mix the almond milk, butter, eggs, and vanilla in another bowl until smooth. 2. Add the wet ingredients to the dry ingredients and stir until just combined, then fold in the blueberries. 3. Divide the batter equally among 12 silicone muffin cups, and place them in the air fryer basket. 4. Bake them in the air fryer at 175°C for 15 minutes until browned and a toothpick inserted in the middle of a muffin comes out clean. 5. Let the muffins cool for 5 minutes after baking. Serve warm or at room temperature.

Per Serving: Calories 150; Fat 4.71g; Sodium 134mg; Carbs 25.69g; Fibre 3g; Sugar 10.02g; Protein 4.95g

Baked Peaches Oatmeal

Prep Time: 5 minutes | **Cook Time:** 10 minutes | **Serves:** 4

Extra-virgin olive oil, in a spray bottle, for greasing
165g oats
½ teaspoon baking powder
1½ teaspoons ground cinnamon
⅛ teaspoon salt
300ml unsweetened vanilla almond milk
80g maple syrup
1 teaspoon vanilla extract
2 peaches, peeled and diced, divided

1. Preheat the air fryer to 175°C. Lightly spray four 150g ramekins with olive oil. 2. Combine the oats, baking powder, cinnamon, and salt in a large bowl, then add the almond milk, maple syrup, vanilla, and three-quarters of the diced peaches, and stir until thoroughly combined. 3. Divide the mixture equally into the prepared ramekins, and bake in the preheated air fryer for 8 to 10 minutes, or until

golden on top and set. 4. Serve with the remaining diced peaches over the top.
Per Serving: Calories 235; Fat 4.78g; Sodium 139mg; Carbs 57.64g; Fibre 9.2g; Sugar 23.73g; Protein 9.18g

Glazed Cinnamon Rolls

Prep Time: 15 minutes | **Cook Time:** 12 minutes | **Serves:** 6

Extra-virgin olive oil, in a spray bottle, for greasing
245g plain Greek yogurt
240g whole-wheat flour, divided, plus more as needed
2 teaspoons baking powder
½ teaspoon salt
95g plus 1 tablespoon sugar, divided
4 tablespoons unsalted butter, at room temperature
2 teaspoons ground cinnamon
100g cream cheese
60ml freshly squeezed orange juice

1. Preheat the air fryer to 175°C. Lightly spray a 20cm baking dish with olive oil. 2. In a large bowl, mix together the yogurt, 210g flour, the baking powder, salt, and 50g of sugar until a sticky dough forms. 3. On a clean work surface, Sprinkle the remaining 30g of flour on the clean work surface, and the place the dough on it and roll into a rectangle about 0.5–cm thick. If the dough is too sticky to roll, add more flour in 1-tablespoon increments until the dough forms. 4. Mix the butter, cinnamon, and 1 tablespoon of sugar in a small bowl. 5. Spread the butter mixture evenly over the rectangle of dough. 6. Starting at the long side, roll the dough away from you, tucking it tightly until a log is formed; cut the log into six equal pieces and place them, cut-side up, in the prepared baking dish so they are touching. 7. Bake them in the preheated air fryer for 10 to 12 minutes until the rolls have risen, are golden brown on top, and are cooked through. 8. Let them cool for 10 minutes after baking. 9. Whisk the cream cheese, orange juice, and the remaining sugar in a separate bowl until a glaze

forms. 10. Pour the glaze over the cinnamon rolls and enjoy.
Per Serving: Calories 305; Fat 12.97g; Sodium 308mg; Carbs 42.36g; Fibre 4.8g; Sugar 11.76g; Protein 8.46g

Peanut Banana Loaf

Prep Time: 5 minutes | **Cook Time:** 35 minutes | **Serves:** 4

90g whole-wheat flour
½ teaspoon salt
¼ teaspoon baking soda
2 medium ripe bananas
2 eggs
95g sugar
75g natural peanut butter, melted
2 tablespoons butter, melted and cooled
1 tablespoon molasses
1 teaspoon vanilla extract

1. Preheat the air fryer to 155°C. Line a 15cm round baking dish with parchment paper. 2. Combine the flour, salt, and baking soda in a small bowl. 3. Mash the bananas with the eggs in a large bowl until well incorporated; add the sugar, peanut butter, butter, molasses, and vanilla and beat until combined; add the flour mixture and mix until incorporated. 4. Transfer the batter to the baking dish and spread in an even layer, and bake in the preheated air fryer for 35 minutes until golden on top and a toothpick inserted in the centre comes out clean.
Per Serving: Calories 375; Fat 16.69g; Sodium 549mg; Carbs 48.4g; Fibre 5.2g; Sugar 19.69g; Protein 12.59g

Whole-Wheat Bagels

Prep Time: 10 minutes | **Cook Time:** 15 minutes | **Serves:** 4

150g whole-wheat flour, divided
2 teaspoons baking powder
½ teaspoon salt
½ teaspoon garlic powder
245g plain Greek yogurt
1 egg
1 teaspoon water
1 teaspoon poppy seeds
½ teaspoon white sesame seeds

½ teaspoon black sesame seeds
½ teaspoon dried minced garlic
½ teaspoon dried minced onion
1 teaspoon coarse salt

1. Preheat the air fryer to 150°C. 2. Combine 120g of flour, the baking powder, salt, and garlic powder in a large bowl; mix in the yogurt until a sticky dough forms. 3. Divide the dough into four equal pieces. 4. Sprinkle the remaining flour on a clean work surface, roll each dough piece into a 15cm log shape on it; join the ends of each dough log to create a circle and pinch the ends together to seal. 5. Beat the egg with water in a small bowl. 6. Whisk the rest ingredients in another small bowl to make the topping. 7. Place the bagels in the air fryer basket, brush the tops with the egg wash and sprinkle with the topping, and then bake them in the preheated air fryer for 15 minutes until golden brown on top. 8. When done, serve and enjoy.
Per Serving: Calories 223; Fat 6.11g; Sodium 933mg; Carbs 35.08g; Fibre 4.7g; Sugar 5.29g; Protein 10.01g

Eggs in Tomato Sauce

Prep Time: 10 minutes | **Cook Time:** 12 minutes | **Serves:** 4
Extra-virgin olive oil, in a spray bottle, for greasing
2 tablespoons tomato paste
120ml chicken stock
4 tomatoes, diced
2 garlic cloves, minced
½ teaspoon dried oregano
½ teaspoon dried basil
¼ teaspoon red pepper flakes
¼ teaspoon paprika
4 eggs
¼ teaspoon salt
¼ teaspoon freshly ground black pepper
2 spring onions, both white and green parts, diced
110g grated cheddar cheese
4 slices sprouted-grain bread, toasted

1. Preheat the air fryer to 175°C. Lightly spray four 150g ramekins with olive oil. 2. Whisk the tomato paste, chicken stock, tomatoes, garlic, oregano, basil, red pepper flakes, and paprika in a large bowl until combined. 3. Divide the mixture into the prepared ramekins and cook in the air fryer for 5 minutes. 4. When the time is up, carefully remove the ramekins from the air fryer, and crack a single egg into each ramekin; top the eggs with a sprinkle of salt, black pepper, and equal amounts of the spring onions and grated cheese. 5. Cook them in the air fryer for 5 minutes more until the cheese is melted and the eggs white is set. 6. Serve warm with the toasted bread for dipping.
Per Serving: Calories 330; Fat 14.52g; Sodium 748mg; Carbs 30.14g; Fibre 5.3g; Sugar 9.88g; Protein 20.64g

Baked Potato Skins

Prep Time: 5 minutes | **Cook Time:** 50 minutes | **Serves:** 4
2 large potatoes
¼ teaspoon salt
¼ teaspoon freshly ground black pepper
1 tablespoon chopped fresh dill
1½ tablespoons butter
2 tablespoons milk
4 eggs
1 spring onion, green part only, sliced
30g grated gouda cheese

1. Poke each potato one two or three times with a fork after washing them. Place them in the air fryer basket or tray, and cook at 200°C for 40 to 45 minutes until tender. 2. Remove the potatoes from the air fryer, and halve them lengthwise; scoop the bulk of the potato out and place in a medium bowl, leaving the skin intact. 3. Add the salt, black pepper, dill, butter, and milk to the bowl, and gently mash them with the potatoes until combined but still a little chunky. 4. Apportion the potato mixture between the potato skin halves, and then create a well in the center of each potato that is at least 1¼cm deep; crack an egg into each halve and top with the spring onions and a bit of grated cheese. 5. Bake them in the air fryer at 200°C for 5 minutes until the egg is cooked

to your preference and the cheese is melted.
6. Serve warm.
Per Serving: Calories 287; Fat 11.74g; Sodium 323mg; Carbs 34.34g; Fibre 4.5g; Sugar 2.2g; Protein 12g

Herbed Vegetable Breakfast

Prep Time: 10 minutes | **Cook Time:** 20 minutes | **Serves:** 4

Extra-virgin olive oil, in a spray bottle, for greasing
6 eggs
½ yellow onion, diced
120g diced mushrooms
2 tablespoons chopped fresh parsley
1 tablespoon chopped fresh chives, plus more for garnish
½ tablespoon chopped fresh dill
60g grated Gruyère cheese

1. Preheat the air fryer to 175°C. Lightly spray a 15cm baking dish with olive oil. Set aside. 2. Beat the eggs in a medium bowl until well combined; add the onion, mushrooms, parsley, chives, dill, and Gruyère cheese, and stir until combined. 3. Pour the egg mixture into the prepared pan, and bake in the preheated air fryer for 20 minutes until the eggs are set in the center. 4. Serve immediately with additional chives over the top.
Per Serving: Calories 167; Fat 10.07g; Sodium 335mg; Carbs 6.36g; Fibre 0.8g; Sugar 2.6g; Protein 12.76g

Crustless Broccoli Quiche

Prep Time: 5 minutes | **Cook Time:** 25 minutes | **Serves:** 4

135g broccoli florets
2 garlic cloves, minced
1 tablespoon extra-virgin olive oil, plus more in a spray bottle, for greasing
½ teaspoon salt, divided
4 eggs
½ teaspoon freshly ground black pepper
2 spring onions, green part only, chopped
1 tablespoon sour cream
60g grated gouda cheese, divided

1. Toss the broccoli with the garlic, olive oil, and ¼ teaspoon of salt in a medium bowl. 2. Line the air fryer basket or tray with parchment paper. Transfer the broccoli to the basket in a single layer. 3. Cook the broccoli in the air fryer at 190°C for 5 minutes. When cooked, set aside. 4. In the same medium bowl, whisk together the eggs, remaining ¼ teaspoon of salt, the pepper, spring onions, and sour cream until the eggs are well incorporated. 5. Add the roasted broccoli, garlic, and 30 g of gouda cheese to the egg mixture and stir until combined. 6. Lightly spray a 15cm baking dish with olive oil, then pour the egg mixture into the dish and top with the remaining 30 g of gouda cheese. 7. Place the dish in the air fryer and cook for 15 to 18 minutes, or until the center is set. 8. Serve warm.
Per Serving: Calories 178; Fat 13.33g; Sodium 500mg; Carbs 4.13g; Fibre 1.3g; Sugar 1.91g; Protein 10.97g

Apple Chicken Sausage

Prep Time: 10 minutes | **Cook Time:** 8 minutes | **Serves:** 6

454g chicken mince
1 medium Granny Smith apple, finely diced
1 garlic clove, minced
1 teaspoon salt
½ teaspoon freshly ground black pepper
½ teaspoon dried sage
¼ teaspoon cayenne pepper
¼ teaspoon fennel seed

1. Preheat the air fryer to 175°C. Line the air fryer basket with parchment paper. 2. Mix the chicken, apple, garlic, salt, black pepper, sage, cayenne pepper, and fennel seed in a large bowl until evenly combined. 3. Divide the chicken mixture into 12 portions, and pat them into 1¼-cm-thick rounds. 4. Place the patties in the basket in a single layer and cook in the air fryer for 7 minutes until they reach an internal temperature of 70°C, turning halfway through. 5. Serve immediately or let cool before storing in an airtight container in the refrigerator for up to 5 days. Uncooked

sausage can be refrigerated for up to 3 days before cooking.
Per Serving: Calories 181; Fat 11.48g; Sodium 441mg; Carbs 4.24g; Fibre 0.9g; Sugar 2.69g; Protein 14.27g

Sirloin Steak and Eggs

Prep Time: 10 minutes | **Cook Time:** 15 minutes | **Serves:** 2

2 tablespoons butter
1 rosemary sprig, divided
200g sirloin steak, fat trimmed
1 teaspoon salt, divided
1 teaspoon freshly ground black pepper, divided
⅛ teaspoon cayenne pepper
Extra-virgin olive oil, in a spray bottle, for greasing
2 eggs

1. Preheat the air fryer to 200°C. Place the butter (in 1-tablespoon pieces) and half the rosemary sprig in the center of a clean cutting board. 2. Lightly season the steak on both sides with ½ teaspoon of salt, ½ teaspoon of black pepper, and the cayenne pepper. 3. Place the steak in the air fryer basket, and top with the remaining half of the rosemary sprig. 4. Cook the steak in the air fryer for 4 minutes. Turn over the steak and cook for an additional 3 minutes. Check the temperature of the meat (60°C for medium, 70°C for well-done). 5. Remove the steak from the air fryer and place on top of the butter and rosemary on the cutting board. Loosely cover with aluminum foil. 6. Spray a 150 g ramekin with olive oil. Crack both eggs into the ramekin and sprinkle with the remaining ½ teaspoon of salt and ½ teaspoon of black pepper. 7. Place the ramekins back to the air fryer, and cook at 190°C for 4 to 5 minutes until the egg white is cooked through. 8. Remove the foil from the steak. Cut the steak into slices and serve alongside the eggs.
Per Serving: Calories 296; Fat 18.93g; Sodium 1429mg; Carbs 1.43g; Fibre 0.5g; Sugar 0.2g; Protein 28.74g

Baked Hard Eggs

Prep Time: 1 minute | **Cook Time:** 15 minutes | **Serves:** 6

6 large eggs

1. Carefully put the eggs in a single layer in the air fryer basket. 2. Bake the egg at 150°C for at least 8 minutes for a slightly runny yolk, or 12 to 15 minutes for a firmer yolk. 3. Prepare a bowl of cold water, and soak the eggs for 5 minutes after cooking. 4. Gently crack the shell under water. 5. Let the eggs stand for another minute or more, then peel and eat.
Per Serving: Calories 72; Fat 4.76g; Sodium 71mg; Carbs 0.36g; Fibre 0g; Sugar 0.19g; Protein 6.28g

Flavourful Asparagus Strata

Prep Time: 15 minutes | **Cook Time:** 17 minutes | **Serves:** 4

6 asparagus spears, cut into 5cm pieces
2 slices whole-wheat bread, cut into 1¼cm cubes
4 eggs
3 tablespoons whole milk
55g grated Swiss cheese
2 tablespoons chopped flat-leaf parsley
Pinch salt
Freshly ground black pepper

1. Place the asparagus spears and 1 tablespoon of water in the air fryer basket. Bake them at 165°C for 3 to 5 minutes or until crisp and tender. 2. Remove the asparagus from the pan and drain it after baking. 3. Spray the pan with nonstick cooking spray. 4. Arrange the bread cubes and asparagus into the pan and set aside. 5. Beat the eggs with the milk in a medium bowl until combined; add the cheese, parsley, salt, and pepper. Pour them into the baking pan. 6. Bake them at 165°C for 11 to 14 minutes until the eggs are set and the top starts to brown. 7. Serve warm.
Per Serving: Calories 230; Fat 14.04g; Sodium 444mg; Carbs 10.13g; Fibre 1.4g; Sugar 2.07g; Protein 15.22g

Prawn Frittata

Prep Time: 15 minutes | **Cook Time:** 15 minutes | **Serves:** 4

4 eggs
Pinch salt
½ teaspoon dried basil
Nonstick cooking spray
60g cooked rice
85g chopped cooked prawns
40g baby spinach
60g grated Monterey Jack cheese

1. Beat the eggs with the salt and basil in a small bowl until frothy. 2. Spray a 12-by-12-by-4-inch pan with nonstick cooking spray. 3. Combine the rice, prawns, and spinach in the prepared pan. Pour the eggs in and sprinkle with the cheese. 4. Bake them at 160°C for 14 to 18 minutes or until the frittata is puffed and golden brown. 5. Serve warm.
Per Serving: Calories 225; Fat 18.01g; Sodium 383mg; Carbs 8.66g; Fibre 3.2g; Sugar 0.88g; Protein 18.37g

Tasty Scotch Eggs

Prep Time: 15 minutes | **Cook Time:** 12 minutes | **Serves:** 6

6 hard-cooked eggs
680g or turkey sausage
3 raw eggs, divided
160g dried bread crumbs, divided
60g flour
Oil, for misting

1. Combine the sausage, one raw egg, and 55g of the bread crumbs in a large bowl. Divide the mixture into six pieces and flatten each into a long oval. 2. Beat the remaining two raw eggs in a shallow bowl. 3. Peel the hard-cooked eggs; roll each hard-cooked egg in the flour and wrap one of the sausage pieces around the egg to completely encircle it. 4. Roll the egg first in the flour, then dip in the beaten eggs, and finally dip in the bread crumbs to coat. Do the same with the remaining eggs. 5. Place the eggs in a single layer in the air fryer and spray with oil. 6. Air-fry them at 185°C for 12 minutes until the turkey is thoroughly cooked and the eggs are brown, turning and misting with more oil halfway through. 7. Serve warm.
Per Serving: Calories 426; Fat 22.36g; Sodium 910mg; Carbs 13.34g; Fibre 0.5g; Sugar 1.41g; Protein 39.72g

Omelet Cups

Prep Time: 12 minutes | **Cook Time:** 11 minutes | **Serves:** 4

4 (7.5-by-10-cm) crusty rolls
4 thin slices Gouda or Swiss cheese mini wedges
5 eggs
2 tablespoons heavy cream
½ teaspoon dried thyme
3 strips precooked bacon, chopped
Pinch salt
Freshly ground black pepper

1. Cut the tops off the rolls and remove the insides with your fingers to make a shell with about 1¼-cm of bread remaining. 2. Line the rolls with a slice of cheese, pressing down gently so the cheese conforms to the inside of the roll. 3. Beat the eggs with the heavy cream in a medium bowl until combined, and then stir in the thyme, bacon, salt and pepper. 4. Spoon the egg mixture into the rolls over the cheese. 5. Bake them at 165°C for 8 to 12 minutes or until the eggs are puffy and starting to brown on top. 6. When done, serve and enjoy.
Per Serving: Calories 348; Fat 20.16g; Sodium 565mg; Carbs 22.54g; Fibre 1g; Sugar 3.16g; Protein 18.41g

Berry Muffins

Prep Time: 15 minutes | **Cook Time:** 15 minutes | **Serves:** 8

160g plus 1 tablespoon flour
2 teaspoons baking powder
50g white sugar
2 tablespoons brown sugar
2 eggs
160ml whole milk
80ml safflower oil
145g mixed fresh berries

1. Combine the flour, baking powder, white sugar, and brown sugar in a medium bowl. 2. Whisk the eggs, oil, and milk in a small bowl, then pour in the flour bowl and stir until combined. 3. Toss the mixed berries with the remaining flour in another small bowl; stir into the batter. 4. Double up 16 foil muffin cups to make 8 cups, arrange 4 cups into the air fryer and fill three-quarter full with the batter. 5. Bake them at 160°C for 12 to 17 minutes until the tops of the muffins spring back when lightly touched with your finger. Do the same with the remaining food. 6. After cooking, cool the muffins for 10 minutes before serving.

Per Serving: Calories 275; Fat 13.65g; Sodium 81mg; Carbs 33.62g; Fibre 1.2g; Sugar 11.72g; Protein 5.07g

Cranberry Beignets

Prep Time: 15 minutes | **Cook Time:** 10 minutes | **Serves:** 16

190g flour
2 teaspoons baking soda
¼ teaspoon salt
3 tablespoons brown sugar
35g chopped dried cranberries
120ml buttermilk
1 egg
3 tablespoons melted unsalted butter

1. Mix the flour, baking soda, salt, and brown sugar in a medium bowl; stir in dried cranberries. 2. Beat the egg with the buttermilk in a small bowl until smooth; stir into the dry ingredients just until moistened. 3. Pat the dough into a 20-by-20-cm square and cut into 16 pieces. Coat each piece lightly with melted butter. Place the dough pieces in a single layer in the air fryer basket, making sure the pieces don't touch. 4. Air-fry them at 165°C for 5 to 8 minutes or until puffy and golden brown. 5. Dust with icing sugar before serving, if desired.

Per Serving: Calories 76; Fat 2.24g; Sodium 216mg; Carbs 11.57g; Fibre 0.3g; Sugar 2.53g; Protein 2.11g

Homemade Pancake

Prep Time: 12 minutes | **Cook Time:** 15 minutes | **Serves:** 4

2 (scant) tablespoons unsalted butter
3 eggs
60g flour
120ml milk
½ teaspoon vanilla
230g sliced fresh strawberries
2 tablespoons icing sugar

1. Preheat the air fryer to 165°C with a suitable baking pan in the basket. 2. Heat the butter in the air fryer until melted. 3. Beat the eggs with flour, milk, and vanilla, in a medium bowl with an eggbeater until combined and frothy. 4. Carefully remove the basket with the pan from the air fryer and tilt so the butter covers the bottom of the pan. Immediately pour in the batter and put back in the air fryer basket. 5. Bake the food for 12 to 16 minutes or until the pancake is puffed and golden brown. 6. Transfer the pancake to a serving plate, top with strawberries and powdered sugar, and enjoy.

Per Serving: Calories 192; Fat 8.31g; Sodium 63mg; Carbs 21.82g; Fibre 1.5g; Sugar 8.32g; Protein 7.31g

Breaded Avocado Fries

Prep Time: 20 minutes | **Cook Time:** 8 minutes | **Serves:** 6

Olive oil
4 slightly under-ripe avocados, cut in half, pits removed
180g of wholewheat panko breadcrumbs
¾ teaspoon of freshly ground black pepper
1½ teaspoons of paprika
¾ teaspoon of salt
3 eggs

1. Spray the air fryer basket lightly with olive oil. 2. Carefully remove the skin from the avocado leaving the flesh intact. Cut each avocado half lengthwise into 5 to 6 slices. 3.In a small bowl, mix together the panko breadcrumbs, black pepper, paprika, and salt. 4. In a separate small bowl, beat the eggs. 5.Coat each avocado slice in the egg and then in the panko mixture, pressing the panko mixture gently into the avocado so it sticks. 6. Place the avocado slices in the fryer basket in a single layer. Lightly spray with olive oil. 7. Air fry them for 6 to 8 minutes at 175°C, turning the slices over and spraying lightly with olive oil halfway through. 8. Serve warm.
Per Serving: Calories 379; Fat 23.14g; Sodium 332mg; Carbs 36.98g; Fibre 10.1g; Sugar 1.13g; Protein 9.67g

Spicy Pickle Fries

Prep Time: 15 minutes | **Cook Time:** 15 minutes | **Serves:** 4

Olive oil
120g of wholewheat flour
1 teaspoon of paprika
1 egg
160g of wholewheat panko breadcrumbs
1 (680g) jar of spicy dill pickle spears

1. Lightly spray the air fryer basket with olive oil. 2. Mix the wholewheat flour and paprika in a small bowl. 3. Beat the egg in another small bowl. 4. Put the panko breadcrumbs in a third small bowl. 5. Pat the pickle spears dry with paper towels. 6. Dip each pickle spear in the flour mixture, then coat in the egg, and finally dredge in the panko breadcrumbs. 7. Place each pickle spear in the fryer basket in a single layer, leaving a little space between each one. Spray the pickles lightly with olive oil. 8. Air fry them at 200°C for 15 minutes, turning the pickles over halfway through. 9. Serve directly after cooking.
Per Serving: Calories 295; Fat 3.78g; Sodium 88mg; Carbs 55.23g; Fibre 4.6g; Sugar 0.46g; Protein 10.93g

Crisp Carrot Chips

Prep Time: 15 minutes | **Cook Time:** 10 minutes | **Serves:** 4

1 tablespoon of olive oil plus more for spraying
4 to 5 medium carrots, trimmed
1 teaspoon of seasoned salt

1. Lightly spray the air fryer basket with olive oil. 2. Cut the carrots into very thin slices. 3. In a medium bowl, toss the carrot slices with 1 tablespoon of olive oil and the seasoned salt. 4. Add half of the carrots to the air fryer basket. 5. Air fry the carrots at 200°C for 10 minutes until crispy, shaking the basket halfway through. The longer you cook the carrot slices, the crispier they will become. Watch closely because smaller slices could burn. 6. Do the same with the remaining carrots. 7. Serve and enjoy.
Per Serving: Calories 55; Fat 3.55g; Sodium 623mg; Carbs 5.84g; Fibre 1.7g; Sugar 2.89g; Protein 0.57g

Spicy Corn on Cob

Prep Time: 10 minutes | **Cook Time:** 16 minutes | **Serves:** 4

Olive oil
2 tablespoons of grated Parmesan cheese
1 teaspoon of chilli powder
1 teaspoon of garlic powder
1 teaspoon of ground cumin
1 teaspoon of paprika
1 teaspoon of salt
¼ teaspoon of cayenne pepper, optional
4 ears of fresh corn, shucked

1. Lightly spray the air fryer basket with olive oil. 2. Mix the Parmesan cheese, chilli powder, garlic powder, cumin, paprika, salt, and cayenne pepper in a bowl. 3. Lightly spray the ears of corn with olive oil and sprinkle them with the seasoning mixture. 4. Place the ears of corn in the air fryer basket in a single layer. 5. Air fry the ears of corn at 200°C for 7 minutes. 6. Turn the corn over and air fry for 7 to 9 minutes more until lightly browned. 7. Serve warm.

Per Serving: Calories 142; Fat 2.7g; Sodium 669mg; Carbs 29.06g; Fibre 4.5g; Sugar 4.76g; Protein 5.72g

Bacon with Brussels Sprouts

Prep Time: 10 minutes | **Cook Time:** 10 minutes | **Serves:** 4

Olive oil
455g of fresh Brussels sprouts, trimmed and
 halved
1 tablespoon of crumbled cooked bacon
2 teaspoons of balsamic vinegar
1 teaspoon of olive oil
1 teaspoon of salt
1 teaspoon of pepper

1. Lightly spray the air fryer basket with olive oil. 2. Toss the Brussels sprouts with the crumbled bacon, balsamic vinegar, olive oil, salt, and pepper in a bowl. 3. Place the Brussels sprouts in the air fryer basket. 4. Air fry

them at 175°C for 10 minutes until they are fork-tender and lightly browned, shaking the basket and lightly spraying with the olive oil halfway through. 5. Serve.

Per Serving: Calories 73; Fat 2.15g; Sodium 644mg; Carbs 11.81g; Fibre 4.5g; Sugar 3.46g; Protein 4.31g

Roasted Tomatoes

Prep Time: 10 minutes | **Cook Time:** 6 minutes | **Serves:** 4

Olive oil
4 Roma tomatoes, cut into 15mm slices
Salt
55g of shredded mozzarella cheese
30g of shredded Parmesan cheese
Freshly ground black pepper
Parsley flakes

1. Lightly spray the air fryer basket with olive oil. 2. Lightly season the tomato slices with salt. 3. Place the tomato slices in the air fryer basket in a single layer. 4. Sprinkle each tomato slice with 1 teaspoon of mozzarella cheese, and top each with ½ teaspoon of shredded Parmesan cheese, then season them with black pepper and sprinkle parsley flakes. 5. Air fry them at 190°C for 5 to 6 minutes until the cheese is melted, bubbly, and lightly browned. 6. Serve warm.

Per Serving: Calories 74; Fat 3.07g; Sodium 261mg; Carbs 5.29g; Fibre 1.5g; Sugar 2.61g; Protein 7.12g

Breaded Bell Pepper Strips

Prep Time: 15 minutes | **Cook Time:** 7 minutes | **Serves:** 4

Olive oil
80g of wholewheat panko breadcrumbs
½ teaspoon of paprika
½ teaspoon of garlic powder
½ teaspoon of salt
1 egg, beaten
2 red, orange, or yellow bell peppers, cut into
 15mm-thick slices

1. Lightly spray the air fryer basket with olive oil. 2. In a medium shallow bowl, mix together the panko breadcrumbs, paprika, garlic powder, and salt. 3. In another small shallow bowl, whisk the egg with 1½ teaspoons of water to make an egg wash. 4. Dip the bell pepper slices in the egg wash to coat, then dredge them in the panko breadcrumbs until evenly coated. 5. Place the bell pepper slices in the fryer basket in a single layer. Lightly spray the bell pepper strips with oil. 6. Air fry them at 200°C for 4 to 7 minutes until lightly browned. 7. Carefully remove from fryer basket to ensure that the coating does not come off. Serve immediately.
Per Serving: Calories 143; Fat 3.03g; Sodium 319mg; Carbs 22.23g; Fibre 1.5g; Sugar 0.27g; Protein 6.03g

Roasted Broccoli

Prep Time: 5 minutes | **Cook Time:** 12 minutes | **Serves:** 4

1½ teaspoons olive oil, plus more for spraying
455g of broccoli
1 tablespoon of everything bagel seasoning

1. Lightly spray the air fryer basket with olive oil. 2. In a large bowl, toss the broccoli with the ½ tablespoon olive oil and everything bagel seasoning. 3. Place the broccoli in the air fryer basket in a single layer. 4. Air fry the broccoli at 190°C for 8 to 12 minutes until they are tender and lightly browned, shaking the basket after 5 minutes of cooking. You can cook them in batches. 5. Serve warm.
Per Serving: Calories 101; Fat 2.63g; Sodium 145mg; Carbs 15.21g; Fibre 4.1g; Sugar 1.93g; Protein 6.09g

Flavourful Broccoli

Prep Time: 10 minutes | **Cook Time:** 20 minutes | **Serves:** 4

½ teaspoon of olive oil, plus more for spraying
455g of fresh broccoli, cut into florets

½ tablespoon of minced garlic
Salt
1½ tablespoons of soy sauce
1 teaspoon of white vinegar
2 teaspoons hot sauce or sriracha
1½ teaspoons honey
Freshly ground black pepper

1. Lightly spray the air fryer basket with olive oil. 2. In a large bowl, toss the broccoli florets with ½ teaspoon of olive oil and the minced garlic, and then season them with salt. 3. Place the broccoli in the fryer basket in a single layer. 4. Air fry them at 200°C for 15 to 20 minutes until lightly browned and crispy, shaking the basket every 5 minutes. Do the same with the remaining broccoli. 5. In a small bowl, whisk together the soy sauce, white vinegar, hot sauce, honey, and black pepper. If the honey doesn't incorporate well, microwave the mixture for 10 to 20 seconds until the honey melts. 6.In a large bowl, toss the cooked broccoli with the sauce mixture, and season with additional salt and pepper, if desired. 7. Serve immediately.
Per Serving: Calories 58; Fat 2.23g; Sodium 229mg; Carbs 7.33g; Fibre 3.2g; Sugar 3.8g; Protein 4.11g

Delicious Broccoli Cheese Tots

Prep Time: 20 minutes | **Cook Time:** 15 minutes | **Serves:** 4

Olive oil
340g of frozen broccoli, thawed and drained
1 large egg
1½ teaspoons of minced garlic
30g of grated Parmesan cheese
30g of shredded reduced-fat sharp Cheddar cheese
60g of seasoned wholewheat breadcrumbs
Salt
Freshly ground black pepper

1. Lightly spray the air fryer basket with olive oil. 2. Gently squeeze the thawed broccoli to remove any excess liquid. 3. Add the broccoli,

egg, garlic, Parmesan cheese, Cheddar cheese, breadcrumbs, salt, and pepper to the food processor, and pulse until it resembles a coarse meal. 4. Scoop up the broccoli mixture and shape into 24 oval "tater tot" shapes. 5. Place the tots in the air fryer basket in a single layer, being careful to space them a little bit apart. Lightly spray the tots with oil. 6. Air fry them at 190°C for 6 to 7 minutes, turn the tots over, and cook for an additional 6 to 8 minutes or until lightly browned and crispy. 7. Serve and enjoy.

Per Serving: Calories 107; Fat 5.71g; Sodium 235mg; Carbs 8.25g; Fibre 2.7g; Sugar 1.56g; Protein 7.23g

Balsamic Asparagus

Prep Time: 15 minutes | **Cook Time:** 10 minutes | **Serves:** 4

4 tablespoons olive oil, plus more for spraying
4 tablespoons balsamic vinegar
680g asparagus, trimmed
Salt
Freshly ground black pepper

1. Lightly spray the air fryer basket with olive oil. 2. Whisk 4 tablespoons of olive oil and balsamic vinegar in a medium bowl to make a marinade. 3. To marinate the asparagus, add them to the bowl and make them be covered by the oil mixture, then wait for 5 minutes. 4. Arrange the asparagus in a single layer in the air fryer, and sprinkle with salt and pepper. 5. Air fry the asparagus at 175°C for 10 minutes until tender and lightly browned. 6. Serve warm.

Per Serving: Calories 168; Fat 13.7g; Sodium 46mg; Carbs 9.34g; Fibre 3.6g; Sugar 5.59g; Protein 3.82g

Roasted Cauliflower

Prep Time: 10 minutes | **Cook Time:** 20 minutes | **Serves:** 4

Olive oil

1 large head cauliflower, broken into small florets
2 teaspoons smoked paprika
1 teaspoon garlic powder
Salt
Freshly ground black pepper

1. Spray the air fryer basket with olive oil. 2. Toss the cauliflower florets with the smoked paprika and garlic powder until well coated, then season them with salt and pepper. 3. Arrange the cauliflower in the air fryer basket, and lightly spray them with oil. 4. Air fry them at 200°C for 20 minutes until nicely browned and lightly crispy, shaking the basket every 5 minutes. 5. Serve hot.

Per Serving: Calories 32; Fat 1.47g; Sodium 60mg; Carbs 4.49g; Fibre 1.8g; Sugar 1.4g; Protein 1.57g

Spinach-Cheese–Stuffed Mushrooms

Prep Time: 15 minutes | **Cook Time:** 10 minutes | **Serves:** 4

Olive oil
100g reduced-fat cream cheese, softened
75g shredded cheese
30g whole-wheat bread crumbs
1 egg
¼ teaspoon salt
¼ teaspoon freshly ground black pepper
25g fresh baby spinach, chopped
20 large mushrooms, stems removed

1. Lightly spray the air fryer basket with olive oil. 2. Use an electric mixer to combine the cream cheese, cheese, bread crumbs, egg, salt, and pepper; add the spinach and stir to combine. 3. Spoon the mixture into each mushroom, pressing the mixture into the mushroom and leaving a little bit popping out of the top. 4. Place the stuffed mushrooms in a single layer in the air fryer basket, then lightly spray with olive oil. 5. Air fry at 185°C for 7 to 10 minutes until the mushrooms have started to brown lightly and the cheese is lightly brown on top. 6. Serve warm.

Per Serving: Calories 225; Fat 17g; Sodium 388mg; Carbs 6.83g; Fibre 1.4g; Sugar 3.85g; Protein 13.18g

Breaded Green Beans

Prep Time: 15 minutes | **Cook Time:** 7 minutes | **Serves:** 4

Olive oil
100g whole-wheat panko bread crumbs
25g grated Parmesan cheese
1 teaspoon garlic powder
½ teaspoon freshly ground black pepper
½ teaspoon salt
1 egg
450g fresh green beans, trimmed

1. Lightly spray the air fryer basket with olive oil. 2. Beat the egg in a small bowl. 3. Mix the panko bread crumbs, Parmesan cheese, garlic powder, black pepper, and salt. 4. Dip the green beans in the whisked egg, and then coat in the panko bread crumb mixture. 5. Place the green beans in a single layer in the air fryer basket, then spritz lightly with olive oil. 6. Air fry the green beans at 200°C for 5 to 7 minutes until light brown and crispy.
Per Serving: Calories 110; Fat 4.98g; Sodium 475mg; Carbs 11.15g; Fibre 2.6g; Sugar 1.57g; Protein 6.23g

Simple Green Beans and Potatoes

Prep Time: 10 minutes | **Cook Time:** 22 minutes | **Serves:** 6

Olive oil
900g new potatoes, each cut in half
2 teaspoons seasoned salt, divided
400g fresh green beans, trimmed

1. Lightly spray the air fryer basket with olive oil. 2. Add the new potatoes to the air fryer basket, and sprinkle with 1 teaspoon of seasoned salt, then lightly spray the potatoes with olive oil. 3. Air fry the potatoes at 200°C for 10 minutes. 4. When the time is up, add the green beans, sprinkle with the remaining 1 teaspoon of seasoned salt, and lightly spray

the potatoes and green beans with olive oil. 5. Air fry them for 8 to 12 minutes until the potatoes are fork tender and lightly browned. If you want the potatoes to be extra crispy, add a few minutes to the cook time and spray with a little extra olive oil. 6. Serve warm.
Per Serving: Calories 133; Fat 0.48g; Sodium 786mg; Carbs 29.68g; Fibre 4.8g; Sugar 1.77g; Protein 3.9g

Crunchy Potatoes

Prep Time: 15 minutes | **Cook Time:** 50 minutes | **Serves:** 4

Olive oil
4 potatoes, peeled
Salt
Freshly ground black pepper
25g grated Parmesan cheese

1. Lightly spray the air fryer basket with olive oil. 2. Make thin parallel cuts into each potato,0.3 cm to 0.6cm apart, stopping at about ½ of the way through. The potato needs to stay totally intact along the bottom. 3. Completely but lightly coat the potatoes with olive oil. 4. Place the potatoes in the fryer basket in a single layer, sliced side up, leaving a little room between each potato. 5. Sprinkle the potatoes lightly with salt and black pepper. 5. Air fry the potatoes at 175°C for 50 minutes until they are fork tender, crispy, and browned, tossing the potatoes and spritzing lightly with more olive oil halfway through. 6. Sprinkle the potatoes with Parmesan cheese and serve.
Per Serving: Calories 195; Fat 1.91g; Sodium 162mg; Carbs 39.37g; Fibre 2.8g; Sugar 1.33g; Protein 6.34g

Delicious Sweet Potatoes

Prep Time: 10 minutes | **Cook Time:** 15 minutes | **Serves:** 4

Olive oil
1½ teaspoon salt
1 teaspoon chili powder
1 teaspoon paprika

1 teaspoon onion powder
½ teaspoon ground cumin
½ teaspoon freshly ground black pepper
¼ teaspoon cayenne pepper
2 large sweet potatoes, peeled and cut into
   2.5cm pieces

1. Spray the air fryer basket with olive oil. 2. Combine the salt, chili powder, paprika, onion powder, cumin, black pepper, and cayenne pepper. 3. In a large bowl, add the sweet potato and spray lightly with olive oil. Add the seasoning mix and toss to coat. 4. Put the sweet potatoes in the air fryer basket. 5. Air fry the sweet potatoes at 200°C for 15 minutes until browned and slightly crispy, shaking the basket every 5 minutes and spraying lightly with olive oil each time. To make them extra crispy, cook for a few more minutes but watch closely to make sure they don't burn. 6. Serve hot.
Per Serving: Calories 64; Fat 0.3g; Sodium 929mg; Carbs 14.63g; Fibre 2.6g; Sugar 2.89g; Protein 1.36g

Cheese Portobello Pizzas

Prep Time: 10 minutes | **Cook Time:** 10 minutes | **Serves:** 4
Olive oil
4 large portobello mushroom caps, cleaned
   and stems removed
Garlic powder
8 tablespoons pizza sauce
16 slices pepperoni
8 tablespoons mozzarella cheese

1. Spray the air fryer basket with olive oil. 2. Lightly spray the outside of the mushrooms with olive oil, and sprinkle with a little garlic powder, to taste. 3. Turn the mushroom over and lightly spray the sides and top edges of the mushroom with olive oil and sprinkle with garlic powder, to taste. 4. Place the mushrooms in the fryer basket in a single layer, top side down. Leave room between the mushrooms. 5. Air fry the mushrooms at 175°C for 5 minutes. 6. Spoon 2 tablespoons of pizza sauce on each mushroom. Top each with 4 slices of pepperoni and sprinkle with 2 tablespoons of mozzarella cheese. Press the pepperoni and cheese down into the pizza sauce. 7. Air fry them for 3 to 5 minutes more until the cheese is melted and lightly browned on top. 8. Serve hot.
Per Serving: Calories 172; Fat 10.45g; Sodium 795mg; Carbs 6.22g; Fibre 0.9g; Sugar 4.67g; Protein 13.39g

Homemade Veggie Burger

Prep Time: 15 minutes | **Cook Time:** 26 minutes | **Serves:** 5
Olive oil
1 medium carrot, chopped very small
Salt
Freshly ground black pepper
200g fresh mushrooms, stems removed,
   chopped very small
1 (375g) can black beans, drained and rinsed
1 egg, beaten
2 tablespoons tomato paste
2 teaspoons minced garlic
½ teaspoon onion powder
¼ teaspoon salt
55g whole-wheat bread crumbs
5 whole-wheat hamburger buns

1. Lightly spray the air fryer basket with olive oil. 2. Place the carrots in the air fryer basket, lightly spray with oil and season with salt and pepper. 3. Air fry the carrots at 175°C for 8 minutes. 4. When the time is up, add the mushrooms to the basket, lightly spray with oil and season with a little more salt and pepper (optional). 5. Air fry them for 5 more minutes. 6. Spread the rinsed black beans out on a paper towel and dry them off, removing as much excess moisture as possible. 7. Mash the black beans in a large bowl; add the garlic, tomato paste, egg, cooked carrots and mushrooms and mix them well. 8. Mash the veggies (optional) and add the bread crumbs. Make the mixture into 5 patties. 9.

Transfer the patties to the air fryer basket, don't let them be overcrowded. Air fry them at the same temperature for 12 minutes, flipping them over and spray them olive oil halfway through. 10. Serve the patties on whole-wheat buns.

Per Serving: Calories 248; Fat 3.49g; Sodium 302mg; Carbs 51.44g; Fibre 7.6g; Sugar 4.3g; Protein 9.35g

Garlic Asparagus

Prep Time: 5 minutes | **Cook Time:** 10 minutes | **Serves:** 4

454g medium-thick asparagus (about 30 stalks), woody ends discarded
2 teaspoons olive oil
⅛ teaspoon salt
1 clove garlic, peeled and minced
2 tablespoons grated Parmesan cheese

1. Preheat the air fryer at 190°C for 3 minutes. 2. Toss the asparagus with olive oil, and then transfer them to ungreased air fryer basket. 3. Cook the asparagus for 9 minutes, tossing halfway through. 4. Transfer asparagus to a large serving dish, and toss them with salt, garlic, and Parmesan cheese until coated. Serve warm.

Per Serving: Calories 54; Fat 3.09g; Sodium 125mg; Carbs 5g; Fibre 2.4g; Sugar 2.14g; Protein 3.25g

Easy Rainbow Carrots

Prep Time: 5 minutes | **Cook Time:** 11 minutes | **Serves:** 4

900g rainbow carrots, peeled, greens trimmed and tops removed, cut lengthwise
1 tablespoon butter, melted
½ teaspoon salt

1. Preheat air fryer at 190°C for 3 minutes. 2. Toss carrots with butter and salt. 3. Add carrots to the air fryer basket, and cook them for 11 minutes, tossing them halfway through. 4. Serve warm.

Per Serving: Calories 118; Fat 3.42g; Sodium 470mg; Carbs 21.73g; Fibre 6.4g; Sugar 10.75g; Protein 2.14g

Blistered Peppers

Prep Time: 5 minutes | **Cook Time:** 8 minutes | **Serves:** 2

150g shishito peppers
1 teaspoon olive oil
1 teaspoon salt, divided

1. Preheat air fryer at 190°C for 3 minutes. 2. Toss peppers with oil and ½ teaspoon salt. 3. Add peppers to the air fryer basket, and cook them for 8 minutes until they are blistered, shaking the basket halfway through. 4. Serve the peppers on a large serving dish, and garnish with remaining salt. Enjoy.

Per Serving: Calories 54; Fat 2.42g; Sodium 1169mg; Carbs 8.05g; Fibre 1.3g; Sugar 4.34g; Protein 1.7g

Buttered Green Beans with Almonds

Prep Time: 5 minutes | **Cook Time:** 12 minutes | **Serves:** 4

30g slivered almonds
260g fresh green beans, ends trimmed
2 tablespoons butter, melted and divided
½ teaspoon salt
¼ teaspoon ground black pepper

1. Preheat the air fryer to 190°C. 2. Place the almonds in the air fryer basket, and cook them for 2 minutes, tossing them halfway through. 3. Transfer them almonds to a small bowl and set aside. 4. Toss the green beans with 1 tablespoon of butter, salt, and pepper, and then transfer them to the air fryer basket. 5. Cook them in the air fryer for 10 minutes, tossing them halfway through. 6. Transfer the green beans to a large serving dish. Serve warm, tossed with remaining butter and garnished with roasted almond slivers.

Per Serving: Calories 69; Fat 6.15g; Sodium 293mg; Carbs 3.59g; Fibre 1.5g; Sugar 0.75g; Protein 0.99g

Simple Fried Broccoli

Prep Time: 10 minutes | **Cook Time:** 10 minutes | **Serves:** 2

1 bunch broccoli (about 340g), 2.5cm trimmed from stalks
2 tablespoons butter, cubed
¼ teaspoon salt

1. Boil a medium saucepan of salted water over high heat, and cook the broccoli in it for 3 minutes. 2. Drain broccoli and transfer to a medium bowl, then toss them with butter and salt. 3. Add broccoli to the air fryer basket, and cook them in the air fryer at 175°C for 6 minutes. 4. Serve warm.

Per Serving: Calories 205; Fat 12.64g; Sodium 393mg; Carbs 20.19g; Fibre 7.9g; Sugar 5.18g; Protein 8.69g

Sesame Carrots

Prep Time: 5 minutes | **Cook Time:** 10 minutes | **Serves:** 4

3 large carrots, peeled, tops removed, and cut into 1¼cm coins
1 tablespoon sesame oil
½ teaspoon salt

1. Preheat air fryer at 190°C for 3 minutes. 2. Toss carrots with sesame oil, and sprinkle them with salt. 3. Cook them in the air fryer for 10 minutes, flipping them halfway through. 4. Serve warm.

Per Serving: Calories 52; Fat 3.53g; Sodium 328mg; Carbs 5.17g; Fibre 1.5g; Sugar 2.56g; Protein 0.5g

Honey Brussels Sprouts

Prep Time: 5 minutes | **Cook Time:** 10 minutes | **Serves:** 4

2 tablespoons balsamic vinegar

1 tablespoon olive oil
1 tablespoon honey
¼ teaspoon salt
⅛ teaspoon ground black pepper
454g Brussels sprouts, quartered

1. Preheat air fryer at 175°C for 3 minutes. 2. Whisk the balsamic vinegar, olive oil, honey, salt, and pepper in a large bowl. 3. Coat the Brussels sprouts quarters with the honey mixture. 4. Cook the coated Brussels sprouts in for 10 minutes, tossing them halfway through. 5. Serve warm.

Per Serving: Calories 102; Fat 3.72g; Sodium 176mg; Carbs 15.98g; Fibre 4.3g; Sugar 8.08g; Protein 3.92g

Healthy Butternut Squash Purée

Prep Time: 10 minutes | **Cook Time:** 25 minutes | **Serve:** 1 cup

1 small butternut squash (about 590g), ends discarded, halved lengthwise, and seeded

1. Preheat air fryer at 200°C for 3 minutes. 2. Add the butternut squash to air fryer basket and cook for 25 minutes. 3. Let the squash rest on the cut board for 10 minutes after cooking. 4. Scoop out flesh and add to a food processor, pulse until smooth. 5. Enjoy.

Per Serving: Calories 19; Fat 0.21g; Sodium 2mg; Carbs 3.95g; Fibre 1.3g; Sugar 2.6g; Protein 1.43g

Simple Roasted Shallots

Prep Time: 10 minutes | **Cook Time:** 10 minutes | **Serves:** 4

8 medium shallots, peeled
2 teaspoons olive oil
¼ teaspoon salt

1. Toss the shallots with olive oil and salt in a medium bowl. 2. Preheat air fryer at 200°C for 3 minutes. 3. Cook the shallots for 10

minutes. 4. Transfer shallots to a medium serving dish and serve warm.

Per Serving: Calories 108; Fat 2.47g; Sodium 154mg; Carbs 20.55g; Fibre 3.7g; Sugar 9.33g; Protein 2.42g

Cheese Courgette Fritters

Prep Time: 10 minutes | **Cook Time:** 22 minutes | **Serves:** 4

250g grated courgette (approximately 1 large)
120g crumbled feta cheese
2 tablespoons minced peeled yellow onion
1 tablespoon gluten-free plain flour
1 tablespoon polenta
1 tablespoon unsalted butter, melted
1 large egg
2 teaspoons chopped fresh dill
¼ teaspoon salt
½ teaspoon ground black pepper
110g plain gluten-free bread crumbs

1. Squeeze grated courgette between paper towels to remove excess moisture, then transfer to a large bowl, and mix with the cheese, onion, flour, polenta, butter, egg, dill, salt, and pepper. 2. Add bread crumbs to a shallow dish. 3. Preheat air fryer to 175°C. 4. Form courgette mixture into twelve balls, approximately 2 tablespoons each. Roll each ball in bread crumbs, covering all sides. 5. Place half of fritters on an ungreased pizza pan. Place pan in air fryer basket and cook 11 minutes, flipping fritters halfway through. Do the same with remaining fritters. 6. Serve warm.

Per Serving: Calories 216; Fat 8.79g; Sodium 535mg; Carbs 25.48g; Fibre 1.8g; Sugar 3.03g; Protein 8.81g

Ears of Corn

Prep Time: 5 minutes | **Cook Time:** 7 minutes | **Serves:** 4

3 large ears of corn, shucked and halved
2 tablespoons butter, melted

½ teaspoon salt
¼ teaspoon ground black pepper

1. Preheat the air fryer to 200°C. 2. Toss corn with the melted butter, and season them with salt and pepper. 3. Add the corn to the air fryer basket and cook for 5 minutes; when the time is up, turn the corn and cook for 2 minutes more. 4. Transfer corn to serving plates and serve warm.

Per Serving: Calories 144; Fat 7.03g; Sodium 308mg; Carbs 20.67g; Fibre 2.9g; Sugar 3.6g; Protein 3.57g

Baked Sweet Potatoes with Brown Sugar

Prep Time: 10 minutes | **Cook Time:** 45 minutes | **Serves:** 2

454g sweet potatoes (about 2 large), scrubbed and perforated with a fork
2 teaspoons olive oil
½ teaspoon salt
2 tablespoons butter
4 teaspoons light brown sugar

1. Preheat the air fryer to 200°C. 2. Rub the potatoes with the olive oil and season them with salt. 3. Place them in the air fryer basket, and bake them for 30 minutes; when the time is up, flip them, and bake them for 15 minutes more. 4. Let the cooked potatoes cool on a cutting board for approximately 10 minutes. Once cooled, slice each potato lengthwise. Press ends of one potato together to open up slice. Do the same with another potato. 5. Garnish each potato with butter and brown sugar. Serve warm.

Per Serving: Calories 461; Fat 16.35g; Sodium 608mg; Carbs 73.5g; Fibre 8.1g; Sugar 11.81g; Protein 7.59g

Dijon Roasted Purple Potatoes

Prep Time: 5 minutes | **Cook Time:** 20 minutes | **Serves:** 4

1 tablespoon olive oil
1 teaspoon Dijon mustard
1 teaspoon lemon juice
2 cloves garlic, peeled and minced
⅛ teaspoon + ¼ teaspoon salt, divided
454g small purple potatoes, scrubbed and halved
2 tablespoons butter, melted
⅛ teaspoon ground black pepper
1 tablespoon chopped fresh thyme

1. Whisk olive oil, mustard, lemon juice, garlic, and ⅛ teaspoon salt in a bowl; cover the bowl and refrigerate the mixture until ready to use. 2. Preheat air fryer at 175°C for 3 minutes. 3. In a large bowl, combine potatoes, butter, remaining salt, and pepper. 4. Place potatoes in the air fryer basket, and cook for 10 minutes; toss them and cook for 9 minutes more. 5. Transfer the potatoes to a large serving bowl and toss with olive oil dressing. Garnish with thyme. Serve warm.
Per Serving: Calories 173; Fat 9.3g; Sodium 144mg; Carbs 20.76g; Fibre 2.7g; Sugar 1.02g; Protein 2.56g

Cream Mashed Potatoes

Prep Time: 10 minutes | **Cook Time:** 15 minutes | **Serves:** 4

454g potatoes (about 2 medium), scrubbed and diced into 2.5cm cubes
2 tablespoons butter, melted
½ teaspoon salt
½ teaspoon ground black pepper
30ml whole milk
60g sour cream
1 tablespoon butter, room temperature
15g chopped fresh dill

1. Preheat the air fryer to 175°C. 2. In a large bowl, toss potatoes with melted butter. 3. Place potatoes in the air fryer basket, and cook them for 14 minutes, tossing them halfway through. 4. Transfer potatoes to a large dish. Mash them with salt, pepper, half of milk, sour cream, and remaining butter. Slowly add remaining milk until desired consistency is reached. 5. Garnish with dill and serve warm.
Per Serving: Calories 193; Fat 10.53g; Sodium 315mg; Carbs 22.43g; Fibre 2.6g; Sugar 2.23g; Protein 3.25g

Red Hassel-backs

Prep Time: 15 minutes | **Cook Time:** 20 minutes | **Serves:** 4

6 baby red potatoes, scrubbed
1 tablespoon olive oil
2 tablespoons butter, melted
1 tablespoon chopped fresh thyme leaves, divided
⅛ teaspoon salt
6 teaspoons sour cream
15g chopped fresh parsley

1. Preheat the air fryer to 175°C. 2. Make slices in the width of each potato about 0.6 cm apart without cutting all the way through potato. 3. Brush the sliced potatoes with olive oil, both outside and in between slices. 4. Place the potatoes in the air fryer basket, and cook them for 10 minutes. 5. When the time is up, brush them with the melted butter, sprinkle them with half of thyme, and cook for 10 minutes more. 6. After cooking. Transfer the potatoes to a large dish, season them salt, top them with dollop of sour cream, garnish with the remaining thyme, and sprinkle with the parsley before enjoying.
Per Serving: Calories 271; Fat 10.29g; Sodium 132mg; Carbs 41.44g; Fibre 4.5g; Sugar 3.34g; Protein 5.28g

Twice-Baked Potatoes

Prep Time: 10 minutes | **Cook Time:** 47 minutes | **Serves:** 4

2 teaspoons olive oil

454g russet potatoes (about 2 large), scrubbed and perforated with a fork

2 tablespoons sour cream

1 (100g) can diced green chilies, including juice

35g finely grated cheese blend

½ teaspoon chili powder

½ teaspoon + ⅛ teaspoon salt, divided

¼ teaspoon ground black pepper

80g canned black beans, drained and rinsed

15g shredded iceberg lettuce

4 grape tomatoes, sliced

15g chopped fresh coriander

1. Preheat the air fryer to 200°C. 2. Rub the potatoes with olive oil, and then place them in the air fryer basket. 3. Cook the potatoes for 30 minutes; flip them, and then cook for an additional 15 minutes. 4. Let the potatoes cool on a cutting board for 10 minutes. Once cooled, slice each potato lengthwise. Scoop out all but a 0.6cm layer of potato to form four "boats." 5. Place scooped-out potato in a medium bowl, add sour cream, green chilies, cheese, chili powder, ½ teaspoon salt, and black pepper. Mash them until smooth. 6. Fold in black beans, evenly distribute mixture into potato skin boats. 7. Place boats back into air fryer basket and cook for an additional 2 minutes. 8. Transfer boats to a large serving plate, and garnish with lettuce, tomatoes, and fresh coriander. Sprinkle tops with remaining salt. Serve warm.

Per Serving: Calories 221; Fat 8.05g; Sodium 803mg; Carbs 33.9g; Fibre 8.6g; Sugar 3.01g; Protein 8.43g

Chapter 3 Snack and Appetizer Recipes

Tasty Pot Stickers

Prep Time: 20 minutes | **Cook Time:** 10 minutes | **Serves:** 10

25g of finely chopped cabbage
15g of finely chopped red bell pepper
2 green onions, finely chopped
1 egg, beaten
2 tablespoons of cocktail sauce
2 teaspoons of low-sodium soy sauce
30 wonton wrappers
3 tablespoons of water, plus more for brushing the wrappers

1. Mix the cabbage, pepper, green onions, egg, cocktail sauce, and soy sauce in a bowl. 2. Place 1 teaspoon of the mixture in the centre of one wonton wrapper, fold the wrapper in half to cover the filling, and then dampen the edges with water and seal well. You can also crimp the edges with your fingers and brush them with water. 3. Add 3 tablespoons of water to the pan under the air fryer basket, transfer the wontons to the basket, and Steam the wontons in 2 batches at 180°C for 9 to 10 minutes. 5. Serve warm.
Per Serving: Calories 293; Fat 1.94g; Sodium 617mg; Carbs 57.16g; Fibre 2.2g; Sugar 0.95g; Protein 10.32g

Special Beef-Mango Skewers

Prep Time: 10 minutes | **Cook Time:** 7 minutes | **Serves:** 4

340g of beef sirloin tip, cut into 25mm cubes
2 tablespoons of balsamic vinegar
1 tablespoon of olive oil
1 tablespoon of honey
½ teaspoon of dried marjoram
Pinch salt
Freshly ground black pepper
1 mango
1. Mix the beef cubes with balsamic vinegar, olive oil, honey, marjoram, salt, and pepper in a medium bowl, and then let them marinate. 2. Cut the mango skin off, carefully cutting around the oval pit to remove the flesh, then cut the mango flesh into 25mm cubes. 3. Alternatively, thread metal skewers, three beef cubes and two mango cubes. 4. Place the skewers in the air fryer basket and grill them at 200°C for 4 to 7 minutes, until the beef cubes are browned and reach an internal temperature of 60°C. 5. Serve hot.
Per Serving: Calories 213; Fat 7.28g; Sodium 88mg; Carbs 18.33g; Fibre 1.4g; Sugar 16.98g; Protein 18.91g

Curried Sweet Potato Fries

Prep Time: 5 minutes | **Cook Time:** 12 minutes | **Serves:** 4

120ml of sour cream
120ml of mango chutney
3 teaspoons of curry powder, divided
230g of frozen sweet potato fries
1 tablespoon of olive oil
Pinch of salt
Freshly ground black pepper
1. Mix the sour cream, chutney, and 1½ teaspoons of curry powder in a small bowl. Set aside for later. 2. Place the sweet potatoes in a medium bowl, drizzle them with the olive oil, sprinkle them with the remaining 1½ teaspoons of curry powder, salt, and pepper, and then transfer them to the air fryer basket. 3. Bake the potatoes at 200°C for 8 to 12 minutes until they are crisp and golden brown, tossing them halfway through. 4. Enjoy the sweet potatoes with the chutney dip.
Per Serving: Calories 255; Fat 7.03g; Sodium 74mg; Carbs 45.09g; Fibre 4.1g; Sugar 2.92g; Protein 4.4g

Kale Chips with Yoghurt Sauce

Prep Time: 10 minutes | **Cook Time:** 5 minutes | **Serves:** 4

280g of Greek yoghurt

3 tablespoons of lemon juice
2 tablespoons of honey mustard
½ teaspoon of dried oregano
1 bunch of curly kale
2 tablespoons of olive oil
½ teaspoon of salt
⅛ teaspoon of pepper

1. Combine the yoghurt, lemon juice, honey mustard, and oregano in a small bowl. 2. Remove the stems and ribs from the kale and cut the leaves into 50 to 75mm pieces. 3. Coat the kale with olive oil, salt, and pepper. 4. Place the coated kale pieces in the air fryer basket and air fry them at 200°C for 5 minutes until they are crisp, tossing them halfway through. 5. Serve the kale with the yoghurt sauce.

Per Serving: Calories 113; Fat 9.18g; Sodium 411mg; Carbs 5.72g; Fibre 1g; Sugar 3.66g; Protein 3.18g

Artichoke Triangles

Prep Time: 15 minutes | **Cook Time:** 9 minutes | **Serves:** 6

1 egg white
55g of minced drained artichoke hearts
3 tablespoons of grated mozzarella cheese
½ teaspoon of dried thyme
6 sheets of frozen filo dough, thawed
2 tablespoons of melted butter

1. Combine the ricotta cheese, egg white, minced artichoke hearts, mozzarella cheese, and thyme in a small bowl. 2. Cover the filo dough with a damp kitchen towel before using to avoid it drying out. 3. Place one sheet of filo dough on the work surface at a time and cut one into thirds lengthwise. 4. Put about 1½ teaspoons of the filling on each strip at the base, fold the bottom right-hand tip of filo over the filling to meet the other side in a triangle, then continue folding in a triangle. 5. Brush each triangle with butter to seal the edges. Do the same with the remaining filo dough and filling. 6. Bake the triangles at 200°C for 3 to 4 minutes until they are golden brown. You can bake them in 3 batches. 7. Serve warm.

Per Serving: Calories 121; Fat 6.64g; Sodium 231mg; Carbs 11.82g; Fibre 1.2g; Sugar 0.73g; Protein 3.51g

Delicious Spinach Dip with Bread Knots

Prep Time: 15 minutes | **Cook Time:** 21 minutes | **Serves:** 6

Non-stick cooking spray
1 (225g) packet of cream cheese, cut into cubes
60ml of sour cream
10g of frozen chopped spinach, thawed and drained
50g of grated Swiss cheese
2 green onions, chopped
½ (310g) can of refrigerated breadstick dough
2 tablespoons of melted butter
3 tablespoons of grated Parmesan cheese

1. Spray a suitable baking pan with non-stick cooking spray. 2. Thoroughly mix the cream cheese, sour cream, spinach, Swiss cheese, and green onions in a medium bowl. 3. Spread the dip into the sprayed baking pan and bake at 160°C for 8 minutes. 4. Unroll six breadsticks and cut them in half widthways to make 12 pieces. 5. Gently stretch each piece of dough and tie it into a loose knot, tucking in the ends. 6. When the cheese dip is done, remove from the air fryer and carefully place each bread knot on top of the dip, covering the surface. 7. Brush each knot with melted butter and top them with the Parmesan cheese. 8. Bake them in the air fryer at 160°C for 8 to 13 minutes until the bread knots are golden brown. 9. Serve warm.

Per Serving: Calories 365; Fat 23.18g; Sodium 597mg; Carbs 29.58g; Fibre 0.8g; Sugar 2.58g; Protein 10.76g

Homemade Arancini

Prep Time: 15 minutes | **Cook Time:** 22 minutes | **Serves:** 6

350g of cooked and cooled rice or leftover risotto
2 eggs, beaten
180g of panko breadcrumbs, divided
50g of grated Parmesan cheese
2 tablespoons of minced fresh basil
16 (20mm) cubes mozzarella cheese
2 tablespoons of olive oil

1. Combine the rice, eggs, 60g of the breadcrumbs, Parmesan cheese, and basil in a medium bowl, and then make them into sixteen 40mm balls. 2. Make a hole in each ball, and insert a mozzarella cube. Form the rice mixture firmly around the cheese. 3. Mix the remaining breadcrumbs with olive oil in another bowl, and then coat the rice balls with them. 4. Air Fry the rice balls at 200°C for 8 to 11 minutes until golden brown. You can cook them in batches. 5. Serve warm.
Per Serving: Calories 331; Fat 17.85g; Sodium 391mg; Carbs 40.36g; Fibre 9.5g; Sugar 2.13g; Protein 13.94g

Pesto Bruschetta

Prep Time: 10 minutes | **Cook Time:** 8 minutes | **Serves:** 4

8 slices French bread, 15mm thick
2 tablespoons of softened butter
110g of shredded mozzarella cheese
115g of basil pesto
200g of chopped cherry tomatoes
2 green onions, thinly sliced

1. Spread the butter on the bread slices, place the bread slices in the air fryer basket with butter-side up, and then bake them at 175°C for 3 to 5 minutes until they are light golden brown. 2. When the time is up, top each bread slice with some cheese, and then resume baking them for 1 to 3 minutes until the cheese melts. 3. Mix the tomatoes, green onions, and pesto in a small bowl. 4. After baking, transfer the bread slices to the serving plate, and top them with the pesto mixture. Enjoy.
Per Serving: Calories 304; Fat 7.11g; Sodium 675mg; Carbs 44.17g; Fibre 2.8g; Sugar 8.59g; Protein 16.98g

Fried Tortellini with Mayonnaise

Prep Time: 10 minutes | **Cook Time:** 20 minutes | **Serves:** 4

170g of mayonnaise
2 tablespoons of mustard
1 egg
65g of flour
½ teaspoon of dried oregano
180g of breadcrumbs
2 tablespoons of olive oil
400g of frozen cheese tortellini

1. Combine the mayonnaise and mustard in a small bowl. Set aside. 2. Beat the egg in another bowl, mix the flour and oregano in a third bowl, and then combine the breadcrumbs with olive oil in a fourth bowl. 3. Dip the tortellini into the egg, then into the flour and into the egg again, and coat them with the breadcrumbs. 4. Air Fry them at 195°C for 10 minutes until they are crisp and golden brown on the outside, shaking the basket halfway through. 5. Serve the tortellini with the mayonnaise.
Per Serving: Calories 500; Fat 28.22g; Sodium 743mg; Carbs 45.96g; Fibre 2.7g; Sugar 1.92g; Protein 15.29g

Breaded Shrimp Toast

Prep Time: 15 minutes | **Cook Time:** 12 minutes | **Serves:** 6

3 slices oof firm white bread
100g of finely chopped peeled and de-veined raw shrimps
1 egg white
2 cloves of garlic, minced

2 tablespoons of cornflour
¼ teaspoon of ground ginger
Pinch of salt
Freshly ground black pepper
2 tablespoons of olive oil

1. Cut the crusts from the bread and crumble them to make breadcrumbs. Set aside. 2. Mix the shrimp with the egg white, garlic, cornflour, ginger, salt, and pepper in a bowl. 3. Spread the shrimp mixture evenly on the bread to the edges, and then cut each slice into 4 strips. 4. Mix the breadcrumbs with olive oil and coat the shrimps with them. 5. Place the shrimp mixture in the air fryer basket in a single layer, and air fry them at 175°C for 3 to 6 minutes, until crisp and golden brown. 6. Serve hot.
Per Serving: Calories 102; Fat 5.02g; Sodium 227mg; Carbs 9.02g; Fibre 1.3g; Sugar 0.75g; Protein 5.09g

Parmesan Hash Brown Bruschetta

Prep Time: 10 minutes | **Cook Time:** 8 minutes | **Serves:** 4
4 frozen hash browns
1 tablespoon olive oil
65g chopped cherry tomatoes
3 tablespoons diced fresh mozzarella
2 tablespoons grated Parmesan cheese
1 tablespoon balsamic vinegar
1 tablespoon minced fresh basil

1. Place the hash browns in the air fryer basket in a single layer. Air-fry them at 200°C for 6 to 8 minutes or until the potatoes are crisp, hot, and golden brown. 2. Mix the olive oil, tomatoes, mozzarella, Parmesan, vinegar, and basil in a small bowl. 3. After cooking, transfer the potatoes to the serving plate, top them with the tomato mixture. Enjoy.
Per Serving: Calories 109; Fat 7.44g; Sodium 56mg; Carbs 9.45g; Fibre 1g; Sugar 0.78g; Protein 1.76g

Waffle Fry Poutine

Prep Time: 10 minutes | **Cook Time:** 17 minutes | **Serves:** 4
115g frozen waffle cut fries
2 teaspoons olive oil
1 red pepper, chopped
2 spring onions, sliced
215g shredded Swiss cheese
120ml bottled chicken gravy

1. Toss the waffle fries with olive oil, and place them in the air fryer basket. 2. Air-fry them at 195°C for 10 to 12 minutes until the fries are crisp and light golden brown, shaking the basket halfway through. 3. Transfer the fries to a suitable baking pan, top them with the pepper, spring onions, and cheese, and then air fryer them for 3 minutes until the vegetables are crisp and tender. 4. Drizzle them with gravy, and cook them for 3 minutes. 5. Serve hot.
Per Serving: Calories 218; Fat 14.83g; Sodium 207mg; Carbs 11.36g; Fibre 1g; Sugar 1.38g; Protein 10.39g

Buffalo Chicken Bites with Blue Cheese

Prep Time: 10 minutes | **Cook Time:** 18 minutes | **Serves:** 4
150g sour cream
60ml creamy blue cheese salad dressing
60g crumbled blue cheese
1 celery stalk, finely chopped
454g chicken mini-fillets, cut into thirds crosswise
3 tablespoons Buffalo chicken wing sauce
100g panko bread crumbs
2 tablespoons olive oil

1. Combine the sour cream, salad dressing, blue cheese, and celery in a small bowl. Set aside. 2. Coat the chicken pieces with the Buffalo wing sauce in a medium bowl. 3. Mix the bread crumbs and olive oil, and then coat the chicken pieces with them, patting each

piece so the crumbs adhere. 4. Air Fry the chicken pieces at 175°C for 7 to 9 minutes until they are golden brown and each chicken piece reaches an internal temperature of 75°C, shaking basket halfway through. 5. Serve the chicken pieces with the blue cheese sauce on the side.

Per Serving: Calories 388; Fat 24.53g; Sodium 490mg; Carbs 13.31g; Fibre 0.5g; Sugar 5.45g; Protein 27.33g

Flavorful Chicken Wings

Prep Time: 5 minutes | **Cook Time:** 25 minutes | **Serves:** 4

8 chicken wings
1 tablespoon olive oil
70g brown sugar
2 tablespoons honey
80ml apple cider vinegar
2 cloves garlic, minced
½ teaspoon dried red pepper flakes
¼ teaspoon salt

1. Cut each chicken wing into three pieces. 2. Toss the wings with the oil before placing them in the air fryer basket; bake the chicken wings at 200°C for 20 minutes, shaking the basket twice while cooking. 3. Whisk the sugar, honey, vinegar, salt, and red pepper flakes in a small bowl. 4. After baking, transfer the chicken wings to a suitable baking pan, and toss them with the sugar mixture. 5. Resume baking the chicken wings at the same temperature for 5 minutes until the wings are glazed. 6. Serve warm.

Per Serving: Calories 218; Fat 5.47g; Sodium 199mg; Carbs 29.79g; Fibre 0.2g; Sugar 28.5g; Protein 13.02g

Easy Potato Chips

Prep Time: 10 minutes | **Cook Time:** 50 minutes | **Serves:** 4

2 large potatoes
½ teaspoon salt

1. Preheat the air fryer to 150°C. 2. Cut 2.5cm off top and bottom of each potato, and thinly slice each potato. 3. Soak the potato slices in a bowl of cold water for 30 minutes. 4. Pat the soaked potato slices dry, and spritz them with cooking spray, and then place them in the air fryer basket. 5. Cook the potato slices for 15 minutes, shaking the basket twice during cooking. 6. When the time is up, increase the temperature to 200°C and resume cooking for 5 minutes more until the potato slices are light brown; sprinkle them with salt. 7. After cooking, place the potato slices on a paper towel and let them cool for 5 minutes. 8. Serve immediately.

Per Serving: Calories 146; Fat 0.15g; Sodium 300mg; Carbs 33.34g; Fibre 2.4g; Sugar 1.14g; Protein 3.95g

Panko Onion Rings

Prep Time: 15 minutes | **Cook Time:** 12 minutes | **Serves:** 4

125g plain flour
1 tablespoon seasoned salt
240ml whole milk
1 large egg
100g panko bread crumbs
1 large onion, peeled and sliced into 0.5cm-thick rings

1. Preheat the air fryer to 175°C. 2. Whisk the flour and salt in a large bowl; beat the egg with milk in a medium bowl; place the bread crumbs in the third large bowl. 3. Coat the onion rings with the flour mixture and set aside for later use, then pour the milk mixture into the flour mixture, and stir them well. 4. Dip the onion rings into the wet mixture, and then coat them with bread crumbs. 5. Place the onion rings in the air fryer basket, and spritz them with cooking spray, cook them for 12 minutes until the edges are crispy and golden. 6. Serve hot.

Per Serving: Calories 211; Fat 3.66g; Sodium 1832mg; Carbs 36.28g; Fibre 1.1g; Sugar 8.52g; Protein 7.4g

Bacon-Wrapped Jalapeño Poppers

Prep Time: 10 minutes | **Cook Time:** 12 minutes | **Serves:** 4

75g full-fat cream cheese
45g shredded sharp Cheddar cheese
¼ teaspoon garlic powder
6 (10cm) jalapeño peppers, trimmed and halved lengthwise, seeded and membranes removed
12 slices bacon

1. Preheat the air fryer to 200°C. 2. Add the cream cheese, Cheddar, and garlic powder to a large microwave-safe bowl, and microwave them for 20 seconds until softened. 3. Stir the cheese mixture well, and then spoon them into the hollow jalapeño halves. 4. Wrap a bacon slice around each jalapeño half, completely covering pepper, then place them in the air fryer basket. 5. Cook them for 12 minutes, turning them halfway through. 6. Serve warm.
Per Serving: Calories 446; Fat 38.81g; Sodium 539mg; Carbs 9.21g; Fibre 1g; Sugar 5.37g; Protein 16.26g

Cream Cheese Wontons

Prep Time: 10 minutes | **Cook Time:** 8 minutes | **Serves:** 4

150g full-fat cream cheese, softened
1 teaspoon garlic powder
12 wonton wrappers
60ml water

1. Preheat the air fryer to 190°C. 2. Mix the cream cheese and garlic powder in a medium bowl until smooth. 3. Place 1 tablespoon cream cheese mixture in the center of one wonton wrapper; brush the edges with water to seal the wonton well, and fold the wonton to form a triangle. 4. Spritz both sides with cooking spray. Do the same with the remaining wonton wrapper and filling. 5. Cook the wontons in the air fryer for 8 minutes until

golden brown and crispy, turning them halfway through. 6. Serve warm.
Per Serving: Calories 367; Fat 7.94g; Sodium 703mg; Carbs 59.6g; Fibre 1.8g; Sugar 2.49g; Protein 12.87g

Lime Tortilla Chips

Prep Time: 5 minutes | **Cook Time:** 5 minutes | **Serves:** 4

8 (15cm) white corn tortillas
60ml olive oil
2 tablespoons lime juice
½ teaspoon salt

1. Preheat the air fryer to 175°C. 2. Cut each tortilla into 4 pieces, and lightly brush them with oil. 3. Place the fillets in the air fryer basket in a single layer, and cook them for 5 minutes, flipping them halfway through. 4. Sprinkle the tortilla chips with the lime juice and salt before serving.
Per Serving: Calories 226; Fat 14.87g; Sodium 313mg; Carbs 22.07g; Fibre 3.1g; Sugar 0.55g; Protein 2.77g

Corn Beef Hot Dogs

Prep Time: 30 minutes | **Cook Time:** 10 minutes | **Serves:** 6

85g polenta
90g plain flour
120ml whole milk
1 large egg
2 tablespoons granulated sugar
2 teaspoons baking powder
6 beef hot dogs

1. Preheat the air fryer to 190°C. Line the air fryer basket with parchment paper. 2. Mix the polenta, flour, milk, egg, sugar, and baking powder in a large bowl, and then let the mixture sit for 5 minutes. 3. Cut each hot dog into four equal pieces, and dip the hot dog pieces into the polenta mixture. 4. Chill them in freezer for 10 minutes, and then place them in the air fryer basket. 5. Cook the bites

for 10 minutes until golden brown, turning halfway through. 6. Serve warm.

Per Serving: Calories 340; Fat 11.14g; Sodium 534mg; Carbs 49.52g; Fibre 1.7g; Sugar 11.37g; Protein 10.28g

Butter Cheese Crackers

Prep Time: 10 minutes | **Cook Time:** 8 minutes | **Serves:** 4

100g sharp Cheddar cheese, shredded
60g all-purpose flour
2 tablespoons salted butter, cubed
½ teaspoon salt
2 tablespoons cold water

1. Preheat the air fryer to 190°C. Line the air fryer basket with parchment paper. 2. Mix all ingredients until dough forms in a large bowl. 3. Pack dough together into a ball and wrap tightly in plastic wrap. Chill them in the freezer 15 minutes. 4. Spread a separate large sheet of parchment paper on a work surface. Remove dough from the freezer and roll out 0.6 cm thick on parchment paper; cut the dough into 2.5cm squares. 5. Place the cracker in the air fryer basket, and cook them for 10 minutes. 6. Let the crackers cool for at least 10 minutes before serving.

Per Serving: Calories 140; Fat 6.48g; Sodium 635mg; Carbs 14.96g; Fibre 0.4g; Sugar 2.05g; Protein 5.46g

Turkey Meatballs

Prep Time: 15 minutes | **Cook Time:** 15 minutes | **Serves:** 5

454g lean turkey mince
50g chopped fresh spinach
30g diced red onion
55g crumbled feta cheese
45g bread crumbs
½ teaspoon salt
¼ teaspoon ground black pepper

1. Preheat the air fryer to 175°C. 2. Combine all the ingredients well in a large bowl. 3.

Make the mixture into about 20 balls, spritz them with cooking spray and place them in the air fryer basket. 4. Cook them for 15 minutes until golden brown and the internal temperature reaches at least 75°C, shaking the basket three times during cooking time. 5. Serve warm.

Per Serving: Calories 223; Fat 10.75g; Sodium 507mg; Carbs 9.77g; Fibre 0.8g; Sugar 1.8g; Protein 21.72g

Homemade Mozzarella Sticks

Prep Time: 10 minutes | **Cook Time:** 2 hours 5 minutes | **Serves:** 4

12 (25g) sticks mozzarella string cheese
130g flour
4 large eggs, beaten
230g panko bread crumbs
2½ teaspoons Italian seasoning
½ teaspoon salt

1. Cut mozzarella sticks in half crosswise. Place them in an airtight freezer-safe bag and freeze at least 1 hour. 2. Add the flour in a bowl, beat the eggs in the second bowl, and mix the bread crumbs, Italian seasoning, and salt in the third bowl. 3. Take out the mozzarella sticks, and dip them in the flour, shaking off the excess; then, dip them in eggs, letting excess drip off, and finally coat them with the bread crumbs. 4. Dip them again in eggs, dripping off excess, and again in bread crumbs so that mozzarella stick is double coated. 5. Arrange the coated cheese sticks on a plate, and refrigerate them for at least 1 hour. 6. Preheat the air fryer to 200°C. 7. Place the cheese sticks in the air fryer basket, and spray them with cooking spray. Cook them for 5 minutes. 8. Let the cheese sticks cool for 5 minutes before serving.

Per Serving: Calories 483; Fat 10.65g; Sodium 1034mg; Carbs 74.03g; Fibre 4.1g; Sugar 4.85g; Protein 20.2g

Lean Pork-Egg Rolls

Prep Time: 10 minutes | **Cook Time:** 17 minutes | **Serves:** 4

225g lean pork minced
3 tablespoons low-sodium soy sauce, divided
½ teaspoon salt
170g broccoli slaw
½ teaspoon ground ginger
8 egg roll wrappers

1. Crumble the pork in a medium skillet over medium heat for 10 minutes until fully cooked and no pink remains. Drain fat and return meat to skillet. 2. Pour 2 tablespoons of soy sauce over the pork, sprinkle with salt and stir. Then, reduce the heat to low and cook for 2 minutes. 3. Add broccoli slaw, pour the remaining soy sauce over the broccoli slaw, and sprinkle with ginger; stir them well and resume cooking for 5 minutes until tender. 4. Preheat the air fryer to 175°C. 5. Position a wrapper so that one corner is pointed toward you. Spoon 3 tablespoons pork mixture across the wrapper near the corner closest to you. 6. Roll the point closest to you over the filling, fold the left and right corners toward the center, then roll the wrapper closed toward the far corner. 7. Do the same with the remaining wrappers and fillings. 8. Place the rolls in the air fryer basket with seam-side down, and cook them for 10 minutes, turning them halfway through. 9. Serve warm.
Per Serving: Calories 266; Fat 3.37g; Sodium 1085mg; Carbs 38.5g; Fibre 1.8g; Sugar 0.14g; Protein 19.85g

Beef Taco Meatballs

Prep Time: 25 minutes | **Cook Time:** 15 minutes | **Serves:** 6

100g Colby jack cheese cut into 1¼-cm cubes
454g lean beef minced
1 (25g) packet taco seasoning
45g bread crumbs

1. Preheat the air fryer to 175°C. 2. Chill cheese in the freezer 15 minutes. 3. Mix the beef with taco seasoning and bread crumbs in a large bowl; make the mixture into about 18 meatballs. 4. Take out the cheese, place on cube into each meatball and roll into a ball. 5. Place the meatballs in the air fryer basket, and spritz them with cooking spray. 6. Cook them for 15 minutes until they are brown, shaking the basket three times during cooking. 7. Serve warm.
Per Serving: Calories 280; Fat 17.71g; Sodium 435mg; Carbs 8.44g; Fibre 0.8g; Sugar 0.96g; Protein 19.94g

Parmesan Croutons

Prep Time: 5 minutes | **Cook Time:** 5 minutes | **Serves:** 4

4 slices sourdough bread, diced into small cubes
2 tablespoons salted butter, melted
1 teaspoon chopped fresh parsley
2 tablespoons grated Parmesan cheese

1. Preheat the air fryer to 200°C. 2. Place the bread cubes in a large bowl, pour butter over them, and add the parsley and Parmesan cheese. Toss them until evenly coated. 3. Place the bread cubes in the air fryer basket in a single layer. 4. Cook the bread cubes for 5 minutes. 5. Serve cooled for maximum crunch.
Per Serving: Calories 442; Fat 7.87g; Sodium 913mg; Carbs 72.48g; Fibre 3.1g; Sugar 6.43g; Protein 15.7g

Russet Potato Skins

Prep Time: 15 minutes | **Cook Time:** 35 minutes | **Serves:** 4

4 large russet potatoes
50g shredded sharp Cheddar cheese
1 teaspoon salt
½ teaspoon ground black pepper
115g sour cream
1 spring onion, sliced

1. Preheat the air fryer to 200°C. 2. Poke several holes in potatoes, and then place them in the air fryer basket. 3. Cook them in the air fryer for 30 minutes until fork tender. 4. Slice the potatoes in half lengthwise and scoop out the insides after cooling them. Maintain the structural integrity of the potato skins. Reserve the potato flesh. 5. Sprinkle the potato flesh with Cheddar, salt, and pepper, and cook then in the air fryer for 5 minutes until cheese is melted and bubbling. 6. Let them cool for 5 minutes after cooking, and then top them with the sour cream and spring onion. 7. Serve and enjoy.
Per Serving: Calories 391; Fat 8.15g; Sodium 715mg; Carbs 69.47g; Fibre 4.9g; Sugar 2.49g; Protein 12.4g

Hot Chicken Wings

Prep Time: 5 minutes | **Cook Time:** 20 minutes | **Serves:** 4

900g chicken wings, flats and drums separated
1 teaspoon salt
½ teaspoon ground black pepper
55g salted butter, melted
60ml hot sauce

1. Preheat the air fryer to 190°C. 2. Sprinkle the wings with salt and pepper, and then place them in the air fryer basket in a single layer. 3. Cook the wings for 20 minutes until the internal temperature reach at least 75°C, and they are golden and crispy, turning them halfway through. 4. Mix the butter and hot sauce, toss the cooked wings with the sauce, and enjoy.
Per Serving: Calories 357; Fat 15.76g; Sodium 1208mg; Carbs 0.79g; Fibre 0.1g; Sugar 0.47g; Protein 50.09g

Korean-Style Chicken Wings

Prep Time: 5 minutes | **Cook Time:** 20 minutes | **Serves:** 4

454g chicken wings, drums and flats separated
½ teaspoon salt
¼ teaspoon ground black pepper
60ml gochujang sauce
2 tablespoons soy sauce
1 teaspoon ground ginger
55g mayonnaise

1. Preheat the air fryer to 175°C. 2. Sprinkle wings with salt and pepper, and then place them in the air fryer basket. 3. Cook the wings for 15 minutes, turning halfway through cooking time. 4. Mix the gochujang sauce, soy sauce, ginger, and mayonnaise in a medium bowl. 5. Toss the cooked wings with the sauce, and adjust the cooking temperature to 200°C, and cook the wings in the air fryer for 5 minutes more until the internal temperature reaches at least 75°C. 6. Serve warm.
Per Serving: Calories 222; Fat 10.28g; Sodium 734mg; Carbs 4.12g; Fibre 0.7g; Sugar 2.46g; Protein 26.72g

Bread Crumbs Fried Pickles

Prep Time: 5 minutes | **Cook Time:** 10 minutes | **Serves:** 4

20 dill pickle slices
110g plain bread crumbs
2 teaspoons seasoned salt
60g plain flour
2 large eggs, whisked

1. Preheat the air fryer to 175°C. Set pickle slices on a paper towel to absorb excess moisture. 2. Combine the bread crumbs and seasoned salt in a bowl, add the flour to another bowl, and add the eggs in the third bowl. 3. Dredge the pickle slice in the flour, shaking off excess, then dip in the eggs, shaking off excess, and finally dip in the bread crumbs. 4. Do the same with the remaining pickle slices. 5. Arrange the pickle slices in the air fryer basket in a single layer, and spritz them with cooking spray. 6. Cook

the pickle slices for 10 minutes until golden brown and crispy. 7. Serve warm.

Per Serving: Calories 120; Fat 2.93g; Sodium 1525mg; Carbs 17.27g; Fibre 1g; Sugar 1.01g; Protein 5.7g

Cinnamon Apple Chips

Prep Time: 5 minutes | **Cook Time:** 15 minutes | **Serves:** 4

2 large Granny Smith apples, cored and sliced 0.3cm thick
¼ teaspoon ground cinnamon

1. Preheat the air fryer to 150°C. 2. Spray apple slices with cooking spray and Place the apple slices in a single layer in the air fryer basket, spray them with cooking spray and lightly sprinkle with cinnamon. 3. Cook the apple slices for 15 minutes. 4. Allow the apple chips cool and continue to crisp up for 5 minutes before serving.

Per Serving: Calories 60; Fat 0.2g; Sodium 1mg; Carbs 14.16g; Fibre 3g; Sugar 9.88g; Protein 0.46g

Broccoli Carrot Bites

Prep Time: 15 minutes | **Cook Time:** 12 minutes | **Serves:** 4

1 (250g) steamer bag broccoli, cooked according to package instructions
50g shredded sharp Cheddar cheese
2 tablespoons peeled and grated carrot
50g blanched finely ground almond flour
1 large egg, whisked
¼ teaspoon salt
¼ teaspoon ground black pepper

1. Let cooked broccoli cool 5 minutes, then wring out excess moisture with a kitchen towel. 2. Mix the broccoli with Cheddar, carrot, flour, egg, salt, and pepper in a large bowl. Scoop 2 tablespoons of the mixture into a ball, then roll into a bite-sized piece. 3. Do the same with the remaining mixture to form twenty bites. 4. Line the air fryer basket with parchment paper, and place the bites on it in a single layer. 5. Cook the bites in the air fryer at 160°C for 12 minutes until golden brown, turning them halfway through. 6. Serve warm.

Per Serving: Calories 166; Fat 6.47g; Sodium 290mg; Carbs 19.37g; Fibre 3.4g; Sugar 2.02g; Protein 8.51g

Bacon-Wrapped Jalapeños

Prep Time: 10 minutes | **Cook Time:** 12 minutes | **Serves:** 4

75g cream cheese, softened
35g shredded mild Cheddar cheese
¼ teaspoon garlic powder
6 jalapeños (approximately 10cm long), tops removed, sliced in half lengthwise and seeded
12 slices bacon

1. Place cream cheese, Cheddar, and garlic powder in a large microwave-safe bowl, and then microwave them for 30 seconds on high, then stir. 2. Spoon cheese mixture evenly into hollowed jalapeños. 3. Wrap each jalapeño half with one bacon slice and secure with a toothpick, covering the jalapeño completely. Do the same with the remaining jalapeño halves and bacon slices. 4. Place them in the air fryer basket, and cook them in the air fryer at 200°C for 12 minutes until the bacon slices are crispy, turning them halfway through. 5. Serve warm.

Per Serving: Calories 153; Fat 11.47g; Sodium 419mg; Carbs 9.21g; Fibre 1.4g; Sugar 4.84g; Protein 5.73g

Cheese-Stuffed Mushrooms

Prep Time: 10 minutes | **Cook Time:** 8 minutes | **Serves:** 10

100g cream cheese, softened
6 tablespoons shredded pepper jack cheese
2 tablespoons chopped pickled jalapeños
20 medium button mushrooms, stems removed
2 tablespoons olive oil
¼ teaspoon salt
⅛ teaspoon ground black pepper

1. Mix the cream cheese, pepper jack, and jalapeños in a large bowl. 2. Lightly coat the mushrooms with olive oil, salt, and pepper, then spoon 2 tablespoons of cheese mixture into each mushroom. 3. Arrange these stuffed mushrooms to the air fryer basket, and cook them in the air fryer at 185°C for 8 minutes until they are golden and the cheese is bubbling, lightly tossing halfway through for even cooking. 4. Serve warm.

Per Serving: Calories 84; Fat 7.58g; Sodium 139mg; Carbs 1.77g; Fibre 0.4g; Sugar 1.19g; Protein 3.1g

Super Easy Pepperoni Chips

Prep Time: 5 minutes | **Cook Time:** 8 minutes | **Serves:** 2

14 slices pepperoni

1. Place the pepperoni slices in the air fryer basket. 2. Cook them in the air fryer at 175°C for 8 minutes until they are brown and crispy. 3. Let them cool 5 minutes after cooking.4. You can store them in airtight container at room temperature for up to 3 days.

Per Serving: Calories 35; Fat 3.05g; Sodium 123mg; Carbs 0g; Fibre 0g; Sugar 0g; Protein 1.6g

Bacon-Wrapped Onion Slices

Prep Time: 5 minutes | **Cook Time:** 10 minutes | **Serves:** 8

1 large white onion, peeled and cut into 16 (0.6cm thick) slices
8 slices bacon

1. Stack 2 slices onion and wrap with 1 slice bacon, and secure them with a toothpick. Do the same with the remaining onion slices and bacon. 2. Place the onion rings in the air fryer basket, and cook them in the air fryer at 175°C for 10 minutes until the bacon slices are crispy, turning them halfway through. 3. Serve warm.

Per Serving: Calories 39; Fat 0.81g; Sodium 213mg; Carbs 2.12g; Fibre 0.3g; Sugar 1.05g; Protein 5.97g

Lemony Shrimp

Prep Time: 5 minutes | **Cook Time:** 6 minutes | **Serves:** 2

1 medium lemon
225g of medium shelled and de-veined shrimps
2 tablespoons of unsalted butter, melted
½ teaspoon of Old Bay seasoning
½ teaspoon of minced garlic

1. Zest the lemon and cut it in half. 2. Place the shrimps in a large bowl and squeeze the juice from ½ lemon over them. 3. Toss the shrimps with the lemon zest and the remaining ingredients, then transfer them to a suitable baking dish. 4. Place the dish in the air fryer basket and cook the shrimps at 200°C for 6 minutes, until they are bright pink. 5. Serve the shrimps with pan sauce.
Per Serving: Calories 157; Fat 8.93g; Sodium 647mg; Carbs 3.03g; Fibre 0.1g; Sugar 0.61g; Protein 16.04g

Cajun Salmon Fillets

Prep Time: 5 minutes | **Cook Time:** 7 minutes | **Serves:** 2

2 x 115g salmon fillets, skin removed
2 tablespoons of unsalted butter, melted
⅛ teaspoon of ground cayenne pepper
½ teaspoon of garlic powder
1 teaspoon of paprika
¼ teaspoon of ground black pepper

1. Brush each salmon fillet with butter. 2. Mix the remaining ingredients in a small bowl and rub the fillet with them. 3. Place fillets in the air fryer basket and cook them at 200°C for 7 minutes until they have an internal temperature of at least 60°C. 4. Serve warm.
Per Serving: Calories 146; Fat 10.02g; Sodium 35mg; Carbs 1.71g; Fibre 0.6g; Sugar 0.29g; Protein 12.27g

Spiced Shrimp

Prep Time: 5 minutes | **Cook Time:** 6 minutes | **Serves:** 2

225g of medium shelled and de-veined shrimps
2 tablespoons of salted butter, melted
1 teaspoon of paprika
½ teaspoon of garlic powder
¼ teaspoon of onion powder
½ teaspoon of Old Bay seasoning

1. Toss the shrimps with the other ingredients in a large bowl, then transfer them to the air fryer basket. 2. Cook the shrimps in the air fryer at 200°C for 6 minutes, turning them halfway through. 3. Serve hot.
Per Serving: Calories 155; Fat 8.94g; Sodium 705mg; Carbs 2.59g; Fibre 0.6g; Sugar 0.16g; Protein 15.85g

Tasty Coconut Shrimps

Prep Time: 5 minutes | **Cook Time:** 6 minutes | **Serves:** 2

225g of medium shelled and de-veined shrimps
2 tablespoons of salted butter, melted
½ teaspoon of Old Bay seasoning
20g of unsweetened shredded coconut

1. Toss the shrimps with butter and Old Bay seasoning in a large bowl. 2. Coat the shrimps with the shredded coconut, and then place them in the air fryer basket. 3. Cook the shrimps in the air fryer at 200°C for 6 minutes, turning them halfway through. 4. Serve hot.
Per Serving: Calories 190; Fat 8.28g; Sodium 228mg; Carbs 1.23g; Fibre 0.4g; Sugar 0.79g; Protein 23.1g

Foil-Packet Lemon Salmon

Prep Time: 10 minutes | **Cook Time:** 12 minutes | **Serves:** 2

2 x 115g salmon fillets, skin removed
2 tablespoons of unsalted butter, melted
½ teaspoon of garlic powder
1 medium lemon
½ teaspoon of dried dill

1. Place each fillet on a 125mm × 125mm square of aluminium foil. Drizzle them with butter and sprinkle with garlic powder. 2. Zest half of the lemon and sprinkle the zest over the salmon. Slice the other half of the lemon and lay two slices on each piece of salmon. 3. Sprinkle the dill over the salmon. 4. Fold the foil to fully close the packets and place the foil packets in the air fryer basket. 5. Cook the fillets at 200°C for 12 minutes, until they can be easily flaked and have an internal temperature of at least 60°C. 6. Serve warm.

Per Serving: Calories 148; Fat 10g; Sodium 34mg; Carbs 2.54g; Fibre 0.3g; Sugar 0.62g; Protein 12.19g

Fish Fingers

Prep Time: 15 minutes | **Cook Time:** 10 minutes | **Serves:** 4

30g of pork rinds, finely ground
25g of blanched finely ground almond flour
½ teaspoon Old Bay seasoning
1 tablespoon coconut oil
1 large egg
455g cod fillet, cut into 20mm strips

1. Mix the ground pork rinds, almond flour, Old Bay seasoning, and coconut oil in a large bowl. 2. Beat the egg in a medium bowl. 3. Dip each fish finger in the egg, and then coat it with the flour mixture. 4. Cook the coated fish fingers in the air fryer at 200°C for 10 minutes, until golden. 5. Serve warm.

Per Serving: Calories 169; Fat 5.81g; Sodium 366mg; Carbs 6.12g; Fibre 0.2g; Sugar 0.07g; Protein 21.67g

Crispy Salmon Patties

Prep Time: 10 minutes | **Cook Time:** 8 minutes | **Serves:** 2

2 x 140g pouches of cooked pink salmon
1 large egg
10g of ground pork rinds
2 tablespoons of full-fat mayonnaise
2 teaspoons of sriracha sauce
1 teaspoon of chilli powder

1. Mix all ingredients in a large bowl and form the mixture into four patties. 2. Place the patties in the air fryer basket and cook them at 200°C for 8 minutes, until crispy, flipping them halfway through. 3. Serve and enjoy.

Per Serving: Calories 325; Fat 25.11g; Sodium 370mg; Carbs 1.21g; Fibre 0.6g; Sugar 0.4g; Protein 22.25g

Crab Legs with Lemon Butter Dip

Prep Time: 5 minutes | **Cook Time:** 15 minutes | **Serves:** 4

60g of salted butter, melted and divided
1.4kg of crab legs
¼ teaspoon of garlic powder
Juice of ½ medium lemon

1. Drizzle the crab legs with 2 tablespoons of butter, and then place them in the air fryer basket. 2. Cook the crab legs at 200°C for 15 minutes, tossing them halfway through. 3. While cooking the crab legs, mix the garlic powder, lemon juice, and the remaining butter in a small bowl. 4. Crack open the crab legs, remove the meat, and dip in lemon butter to enjoy.

Per Serving: Calories 393; Fat 9.25g; Sodium 1862mg; Carbs 2.8g; Fibre 51.6g; Sugar 21.42g; Protein 26.06g

Delicious Firecracker Shrimp

Prep Time: 10 minutes | **Cook Time:** 7 minutes | **Serves:** 4

455g of medium shelled and de-veined shrimps
2 tablespoons of salted butter, melted
½ teaspoon of Old Bay seasoning
¼ teaspoon of garlic powder
2 tablespoons of sriracha sauce
¼ teaspoon of powdered erythritol
55g of full-fat mayonnaise
⅛ teaspoon of ground black pepper

1. Toss the shrimps with the butter, Old Bay seasoning, and garlic powder, and then transfer them to the air fryer basket. 2. Cook the shrimps at 200°C for 7 minutes, until they are bright pink, flipping them halfway through. 3. Mix the sriracha sauce, powdered erythritol, mayonnaise, and pepper in a large bowl, then toss in the cooked shrimps. Enjoy.
Per Serving: Calories 157; Fat 5.5g; Sodium 230mg; Carbs 2.8g; Fibre 0.7g; Sugar 0.83g; Protein 24.85g

Foil-Packet Lobster Tail with Parsley

Prep Time: 15 minutes | **Cook Time:** 12 minutes | **Serves:** 2

2 x 170g lobster tails, halved
2 tablespoons of salted butter, melted
½ teaspoon of Old Bay seasoning
Juice of ½ medium lemon
1 teaspoon of dried parsley

1. Place the two halved tails on a sheet of aluminium foil and drizzle them with butter, Old Bay seasoning, and lemon juice. 2. Seal the foil packets, covering the tails completely, and then place them in the air fryer basket. 3. Cook the tails at 190°C for 12 minutes. 4. After cooking, sprinkle the tails with dried parsley, and serve immediately.

Per Serving: Calories 136; Fat 8.31g; Sodium 422mg; Carbs 0.99g; Fibre 0.1g; Sugar 0.31g; Protein 26.06g

Tuna Courgette Casserole

Prep Time: 15 minutes | **Cook Time:** 15 minutes | **Serves:** 4

2 tablespoons salted butter
15g diced white onion
20g chopped white mushrooms
2 stalks celery, finely chopped
120g heavy cream
120ml vegetable stock
2 tablespoons full-fat mayonnaise
¼ teaspoon xanthan gum
½ teaspoon red pepper flakes
2 medium courgettes, spiralized
2 (125 g) cans albacore tuna

1. Melt the butter in a large saucepan over medium heat; add onion, mushrooms, and celery, and sauté them for 3 to 5 minutes until fragrant. 2. After pouring in the heave cream, vegetable stock, mayonnaise, and xanthan gum, reduce the heat and resume cooking for 3 minutes until the mixture begins to thicken. 3. Add the red pepper flakes, courgette, and tuna, then turn off the heat and stir them until courgette noodles are coated. 4. Transfer the mixture to a round baking dish with 4 cups, and cover the dish with foil, then place the baking dish in the air fryer basket. 5. Cook the food in the air fryer at 185°C for 15 minutes. 6. After 12 minutes of cooking, remove the foil and cook the top until browned. 7. Serve warm.
Per Serving: Calories 198; Fat 17.43g; Sodium 288mg; Carbs 2.81g; Fibre 0.5g; Sugar 1.63g; Protein 8.35g

Cream Prawn Scampi

Prep Time: 10 minutes | **Cook Time:** 8 minutes | **Serves:** 4

4 tablespoons salted butter
½ medium lemon

1 teaspoon minced roasted garlic
60g heavy whipping cream
¼ teaspoon xanthan gum
¼ teaspoon red pepper flakes
454g medium peeled and deveined prawns
1 tablespoon chopped fresh parsley

1. Zest the lemon. 2. Melt the butter in a medium saucepan over medium heat, melt butter, then squeeze juice into the pan. 3. Add the garlic, cream, xanthan gum, and red pepper flakes to the pan, cook them for 2 to 3 minutes until the mixture begins thicken, whisking regularly. 4. Place the prawns to a round baking dish, pour them with the cream sauce, and then cover the dish with foil. Place the baking dish in the air fryer basket. 5. Cook the prawns in the air fryer at 200°C for 8 minutes, stirring them twice during cooking. 6. Garnish with parsley after cooking, and then serve warm.
Per Serving: Calories 178; Fat 11.58g; Sodium 288mg; Carbs 2.29g; Fibre 0.1g; Sugar 0.57g; Protein 15.82g

Fried Tuna Avocado Balls

Prep Time: 10 minutes | **Cook Time:** 7 minutes | **Serves:** 4

1 (250g) can tuna, drained
55g full-fat mayonnaise
1 stalk celery, chopped
1 medium avocado, peeled, pitted, and mashed
50g finely ground almond flour, divided
2 teaspoons coconut oil

1. Mix tuna, mayonnaise, celery, and mashed avocado in a bowl, then make the mixture into balls. 2. Coat the balls in almond flour and spritz them with coconut oil, then place them in the air fryer basket. 3. Cook the balls at 200°C for 7 minutes; after 5 minutes of cooking time, turn the balls. 4. Serve warm.
Per Serving: Calories 541; Fat 11.54g; Sodium 183mg; Carbs 18.18g; Fibre 4.4g; Sugar 0.82g; Protein 18.24g

Fish Vegetable Bowl

Prep Time: 10 minutes | **Cook Time:** 10 minutes | **Serves:** 2

170g shredded cabbage
60g full-fat sour cream
2 tablespoons full-fat mayonnaise
25g chopped pickled jalapeños
2 (75g) cod fillets
1 teaspoon chili powder
1 teaspoon cumin
½ teaspoon paprika
¼ teaspoon garlic powder
1 medium avocado, peeled, pitted, and sliced
½ medium lime

1. Coat the cabbage with sour cream, mayonnaise, and jalapeños in a large bowl, and then refrigerate them for 20 minutes. 2. Sprinkle the cod fillets with chili powder, cumin, paprika, and garlic powder, and then place them in the air fryer basket. 3. Cook the fillets at 185°C for 10 minutes until they have and internal temperature of 60°C, flipping them halfway through. 4. Apportion the slaw mixture between two serving bowls, break the cod fillets into pieces and spread over the bowls, top them with avocado, and squeeze with lime juice. Enjoy.
Per Serving: Calories 293; Fat 21.5g; Sodium 350mg; Carbs 19.13g; Fibre 8.6g; Sugar 2.93g; Protein 10.67g

Spiced Crab Dip

Prep Time: 10 minutes | **Cook Time:** 8 minutes | **Serves:** 4

200g full-fat cream cheese, softened
55g full-fat mayonnaise
60g full-fat sour cream
1 tablespoon lemon juice
½ teaspoon hot sauce
20g chopped pickled jalapeños
15g sliced spring onion
2 (150g) cans crabmeat
50g shredded Cheddar cheese

1. Place all ingredients into a round baking dish, and stir until fully combined. Place the baking dish into the air fryer basket. 2. Cook the food at 200°C for 8 minutes until hot. 3. Serve warm.

Per Serving: Calories 308; Fat 17.17g; Sodium 800mg; Carbs 14.21g; Fibre 0.7g; Sugar 7.35g; Protein 24.17g

Almond Salmon Fillets

Prep Time: 5 minutes | **Cook Time:** 12 minutes | **Serves:** 2

60g pesto
35g sliced almonds, roughly chopped
2 (3.8cm-thick) salmon fillets (about 100g each)
2 tablespoons unsalted butter, melted

1. Mix the pesto and almonds in a small bowl. Set aside. 2. Place the fillets into a suitable round baking dish. 3. Brush each fillet with butter, and top each fillet with half of the pesto mixture. 4. Place the baking dish in the air fryer basket. 5. Cook the fillets at 200°C for 12 minutes until they easily flake and have an internal temperature of at least 60°C. 6. Serve warm.

Per Serving: Calories 372; Fat 29.08g; Sodium 341mg; Carbs 1.27g; Fibre 0.3g; Sugar 0.26g; Protein 26.36g

Mayonnaise Crab Cakes

Prep Time: 10 minutes | **Cook Time:** 10 minutes | **Serves:** 4

2 (150g) cans crabmeat
25g finely ground almond flour
1 large egg
2 tablespoons full-fat mayonnaise
½ teaspoon Dijon mustard
½ tablespoon lemon juice
½ medium green pepper, seeded and chopped
15g chopped spring onion
½ teaspoon Old Bay seasoning

1. Combine all ingredients in a large bowl, then form the mixture into four balls and flatten into patties. 2. Place the patties in the air fryer basket, and cook the mixture at 175°C for 10 minutes. 3. Flip the patties halfway through. 4. Serve warm.

Per Serving: Calories 113; Fat 4.64g; Sodium 325mg; Carbs 7.07g; Fibre 0.4g; Sugar 0.58g; Protein 10.2g

Coriander Baked Salmon

Prep Time: 10 minutes | **Cook Time:** 12 minutes | **Serves:** 2

2 (75g) salmon fillets, skin removed
1 tablespoon salted butter, melted
1 teaspoon chili powder
½ teaspoon finely minced garlic
25g sliced pickled jalapeños
½ medium lime, juiced
2 tablespoons chopped coriander

1. Place the salmon fillets in a suitable round baking pan. 2. Brush each fillet with butter, sprinkle with chili powder and garlic, and then place jalapeño slices on top and around the fillets. Place the baking pan in the air fryer basket. 3. Cook the fillets at 185°C for 12 minutes until they flake easily and reach an internal temperature of at least 60°C. 4. After cooking, spritz the fillets with the remaining lime juice and garnish with coriander. Enjoy.

Per Serving: Calories 95; Fat 5.68g; Sodium 237mg; Carbs 2.3g; Fibre 0.7g; Sugar 0.49g; Protein 8.99g

Sesame Tuna Steak

Prep Time: 5 minutes | **Cook Time:** 8 minutes | **Serves:** 2

2 (150g) tuna steaks
1 tablespoon coconut oil, melted
½ teaspoon garlic powder
2 teaspoons white sesame seeds
2 teaspoons black sesame seeds

1. Brush each tuna steak with coconut oil and sprinkle them with garlic powder. 2. Mix the white and black sesame seeds and then press each tuna steak into them, covering the steak as completely as possible. Place tuna steaks in the air fryer basket. 3. Cook the tuna steak at 200°C for 8 minutes until they have an internal temperature of 60°C, flipping them halfway through. 4. Serve warm

Per Serving: Calories 188; Fat 10.53g; Sodium 41mg; Carbs 1.22g; Fibre 0.7g; Sugar 0.05g; Protein 21.99g

Salmon Jerky

Prep Time: 5 minutes | **Cook Time:** 4 hours | **Serves:** 4

454g salmon, skin and bones removed
60ml soy sauce (or liquid aminos)
½ teaspoon liquid smoke
¼ teaspoon ground black pepper
Juice of ½ medium lime
½ teaspoon ground ginger
¼ teaspoon red pepper flakes

1. Slice the salmon into 0.6cm-thick and 10cm long slices. 2. Place the salmon pieces into a large storage bag, and mix with the remaining ingredients. Allow them to marinate for 2 hours in the refrigerator. 3. Place the salmon pieces in the air fryer basket in a single layer, and then cook them at 60°C for 4 hours. 5. Cool them after cooking, and then store them in a sealed container until ready to eat.

Per Serving: Calories 195; Fat 7.93g; Sodium 327mg; Carbs 5.12g; Fibre 0.5g; Sugar 3.46g; Protein 24.55g

Prawn-Vegetable Kebabs

Prep Time: 10 minutes | **Cook Time:** 7 minutes | **Serves:** 2

18 medium shelled and deveined prawns
1 medium courgette, cut into 2.5cm cubes
½ medium red pepper, cut into 2.5cm thick squares

15g medium red onion, cut into 2.5cm thick squares
1½ tablespoons coconut oil, melted
2 teaspoons chili powder
½ teaspoon paprika
¼ teaspoon ground black pepper

1. Soak four 6" bamboo skewers in water for 30 minutes. 2. Alternatively thread a prawn, a courgette, a pepper, and an onion on the skewer. Repeat until all ingredients are utilized. 3. Brush each kebab with coconut oil, sprinkle with chili powder, paprika, and black pepper, and then place them in the air fryer basket. 4. Cook the skewers at 200°C for 7 minutes or until shrimp is fully cooked and veggies are tender, flipping them halfway through. 5.Serve warm.

Per Serving: Calories 149; Fat 11.28g; Sodium 385mg; Carbs 5.21g; Fibre 1.7g; Sugar 1.7g; Protein 8.44g

Easy Buttery Cod

Prep Time: 5 minutes | **Cook Time:** 8 minutes | **Serves:** 2

2 (100g) cod fillets
2 tablespoons salted butter, melted
1 teaspoon Old Bay seasoning
½ medium lemon, sliced

1. Place cod fillets in a suitable round baking dish. 2. Brush each fillet with butter, and sprinkle with Old Bay seasoning. Lay two lemon slices on each fillet. 3. Cover the baking dish with foil, and place into the air fryer basket. 4. Cook the fillets at 175°C for 8 minutes until they have an internal temperature of 60°C, flipping them halfway through. 5. Serve warm.

Per Serving: Calories 110; Fat 7.91g; Sodium 234mg; Carbs 1.06g; Fibre 0.1g; Sugar 0.31g; Protein 8.8g

Lemon Crab-Stuffed Mushrooms

Prep Time: 10 minutes | **Cook Time:** 20 minutes | **Serves:** 6

50g cream cheese, at room temperature
85g crabmeat, shells discarded
1 teaspoon prepared horseradish
1 teaspoon lemon juice
½ teaspoon salt
½ teaspoon freshly ground black pepper
400g cremini mushrooms, stems removed
2 tablespoons panko bread crumbs
2 tablespoons butter, melted
15g chopped fresh parsley

1. Preheat the air fryer to 175°C. 2. Combine the cream cheese, crabmeat, horseradish, lemon juice, salt, and pepper in a bowl, and then evenly stuff the mushroom caps with the cream cheese mixture into mushroom caps. 3. Distribute bread crumbs over stuffed mushrooms, and drizzle melted butter over bread crumbs. 4. Place half of mushrooms in the air fryer basket, and cook them for 10 minutes. 5. Transfer them to the serving plate after cooking. Do the same with the remaining mushrooms. 6. Garnish the dish with chopped parsley, and enjoy.
Per Serving: Calories 126; Fat 7.57g; Sodium 351mg; Carbs 11.37g; Fibre 1.4g; Sugar 2.81g; Protein 4.56g

Tasty Steamer Clams

Prep Time: 20 minutes | **Cook Time:** 7 minutes | **Serves:** 2

25 littleneck clams, scrubbed
2 tablespoons water
2 tablespoons butter, melted
2 lemon wedges

1. Place clams in a large bowl filled with water. Let stand for 10 minutes. 2. Drain them, then refill the bowl with water and let them stand for 10 minutes more. Drain them. 2. Preheat air fryer to 350 °F/ 175°C. 3. Pour 2 tablespoons water in air fryer, add the clams to the air fryer basket, and cook them for 7 minutes. Discard any clams that don't open. 4. Remove clams from shells and add to a large serving dish with melted butter. Squeeze lemon on top and serve.
Per Serving: Calories 236; Fat 9.57g; Sodium 1095mg; Carbs 9.78g; Fibre 0.1g; Sugar 1.21g; Protein 27.22g

Butter Bay Scallops

Prep Time: 5 minutes | **Cook Time:** 5 minutes | **Serves:** 4

2 tablespoons butter, melted
Juice from 1 medium lime
¼ teaspoon salt
454g bay scallops

1. Preheat air fryer to 350°F/ 175°C. 2. Coat the scallops with butter, lime juice, and salt in a medium bowl. 3. Transfer the scallops to the air fryer basket, and cook them for 5 minutes, stirring them halfway through. 4. Serve warm.
Per Serving: Calories 116; Fat 4.42g; Sodium 593mg; Carbs 4.53g; Fiber 0g; Sugar 0.19g; Protein 13.95g

Smoky Calamari Rings

Prep Time: 15 minutes | **Cook Time:** 8 minutes | **Serves:** 4

2 tablespoons no-sugar-added tomato paste
1 tablespoon gochujang
1 tablespoon fresh lime juice
1 teaspoon smoked paprika
½ teaspoon salt
165g crushed pork rinds
150g (about 6) calamari tubes, cut into ¼" rings

1. Preheat air fryer to 400°F/ 200°C. Lightly grease the air fryer basket with oil. 2. Whisk the tomato paste, gochujang, lime juice, paprika, and salt in a medium bowl. 3. Add pork rinds to a separate shallow dish. 4. Dredge a

calamari ring in tomato mixture, shaking off any excess, and then roll it through the pork rind crumbs. Do the same with the remaining rings. 5. Place the calamari rings in air fryer basket, and cook them for 4 minutes, turning them halfway through. You can cook them in 2 batches. 6. Serve warm.

Per Serving: Calories 282; Fat 25.95g; Sodium 614mg; Carbs 2.75g; Fiber 0.6g; Sugar 1.27g; Protein 9.32g

Breaded Fish Sticks

Prep Time: 10 minutes | **Cook Time:** 20 minutes | **Serves:** 4

For Tartar Sauce
115g mayonnaise
1 tablespoon Dijon mustard
65g small-diced dill pickles
⅛ teaspoon salt
¼ teaspoon freshly ground black pepper
For Fish Sticks
1 large egg, beaten
30g arrowroot flour
24g almond flour
½ teaspoon salt
¼ teaspoon freshly ground black pepper
454g cod, cut into 1" sticks

1. To make the tartar sauce, mix all the tartar sauce ingredients in a small bowl, cover the bowl and refrigerate the mixture for serving. 2. To make the fish sticks: Preheat the air fryer to 350°F/ 175°C. Lightly grease the air fryer basket. 3. Place the egg in a small bowl; combine the arrowroot flour, almond flour, salt and pepper in a separate shallow dish. 4. Dip a fish stick into the egg, shaking off any excess egg, and roll in the flour mixture, then place on a large plate. 5. Do the same with the remaining fish sticks. 6. Place the fish sticks in the air fryer basket, and cook them for 10 minutes, turning halfway through. You can cook them in 2 batches. 7. Serve warm with tartar sauce on the side.

Per Serving: Calories 227; Fat 11.43g; Sodium 1149mg; Carbs 8.96g; Fiber 1g; Sugar 0.53g; Protein 20.98g

Crab Cakes with Watercress Salad

Prep Time: 15 minutes | **Cook Time:** 10 minutes | **Serves:** 2

For Crab Cakes
235g lump crabmeat, shells discarded
2 tablespoons mayonnaise
½ teaspoon Dijon mustard
½ teaspoon lemon juice
2 teaspoons peeled and minced onion
¼ teaspoon prepared horseradish
25g ground almond
1 large egg white, beaten
½ teaspoon Old Bay Seasoning (or Season All)
For Salad
1 tablespoon olive oil
2 teaspoons lemon juice
⅛ teaspoon salt
⅛ teaspoon freshly ground black pepper
119g fresh watercress
72g fresh blackberries
30g walnut pieces
2 lemon wedges

1. To make crab cakes: Preheat the air fryer at 400°F/ 200°C for 3 minutes. Lightly grease the air fryer basket with oil. 2. Combine all ingredients, and then form the mixture into four patties. 3. Place the patties into air fryer basket, and cook them for 10 minutes, turning them halfway through. 4. Transfer the crab cakes to a large plate. Set aside. 5. To make the salad: Toss the watercress with olive oil, lemon juice, salt and pepper in a large bowl. 6. Place the salad into two medium bowls. 7. Add two crab cakes to each bowl, garnish them with blackberries, walnuts, and lemon wedges. Enjoy!

Per Serving: Calories 431; Fat 20.38g; Sodium 690mg; Carbs 36.68g; Fiber 7g; Sugar 21.48g; Protein 29.61g

Bacon Stuffed Prawns

Prep Time: 10 minutes | **Cook Time:** 18 minutes | **Serves:** 4

454g (about 20) large raw prawns, deveined and shelled
3 tablespoons crumbled goat cheese
2 tablespoons panko breadcrumbs
¼ teaspoon Worcestershire sauce
½ teaspoon prepared horseradish
¼ teaspoon garlic powder
2 teaspoons mayonnaise
¼ teaspoon freshly ground black pepper
2 tablespoons water
5 slices bacon, quartered
15g chopped fresh parsley

1. Butterfly the prawns by cutting down the spine of each prawn, without going all the way through. 2. Combine the goat cheese, breadcrumbs, Worcestershire sauce, horse-radish, garlic powder, mayonnaise, and pepper in a medium bowl. 3. Preheat air fryer at 400°F/ 200°C for 3 minutes. Pour 2 tablespoons of water in the air fryer basket. 4. Evenly press the goat cheese mixture into the prawns; wrap a piece of bacon around each piece of prawn to hold in cheese mixture. 5. Place half of prawns in the air fryer basket, cook them for 9 minutes, turning them halfway through. 6. Garnish the prawns with chopped parsley after cooking. Serve warm.
Per Serving: Calories 286; Fat 16.79g; Sodium 526mg; Carbs 4.41g; Fiber 0.4g; Sugar 1.46g; Protein 29.51g

Easy Raw Prawn

Prep Time: 5 minutes | **Cook Time:** 6 minutes | **Serves:** 2

454g medium raw prawns, tail on, deveined, and thawed or fresh
2 tablespoons butter, melted
1 tablespoon fresh lemon juice (about ½ medium lemon)

1. Preheat air fryer to 175°C. Lightly grease the air fryer basket with olive oil. 2. Toss the prawns with butter in a large bowl. 3. Transfer the prawns to the air fryer basket, and cook them for 6 minutes; after 4 minutes of cooking time, flipping the prawns and resume cooking. 4. Transfer the prawns to a large serving plate, squeeze lemon juice over them, and enjoy.
Per Serving: Calories 264; Fat 8.89g; Sodium 275mg; Carbs 0.53g; Fibre 0g; Sugar 0.19g; Protein 46.08g

Lime–Crusted Halibut Fillets

Prep Time: 10 minutes | **Cook Time:** 10 minutes | **Serves:** 2

2 tablespoons butter, melted
50g grated parmesan
2 (150g) halibut fillets

1. Preheat air fryer to 175°C. Lightly grease the air fryer basket with olive oil. 2. Combine the butter and parmesan in a small bowl, then press the mixture onto the tops of halibut fillets. 3. Place the fillets to the air fryer basket, and cook them in the air fryer for 10 minutes until they are opaque and flake easily with a fork. 4. Serve warm.
Per Serving: Calories 275; Fat 23.33g; Sodium 161mg; Carbs 5.1g; Fibre 0.2g; Sugar 1.03g; Protein 12.6g

Tuna Croquettes with Dill

Prep Time: 15 minutes | **Cook Time:** 24 minutes | **Serves:** 4

1 (300g) can tuna in water, drained
70g mayonnaise
1 tablespoon minced fresh celery
2 teaspoons dried dill, divided
1 teaspoon fresh lime juice
100g grated parmesan
1 large egg
1 teaspoon prepared horseradish

1. Preheat air fryer to 190°C. Lightly grease the air fryer basket with olive oil. 2. Combine the tuna, mayonnaise, celery, 1 teaspoon dill, lime juice, 25g parmesan, egg, and horseradish in a medium bowl, then form the mixture into twelve rectangular mound shapes. 3. Roll each croquette in a shallow dish with the remaining grated parmesan. 4. Working in 2 batches, cook the croquettes for 4 minutes, turn ⅓ of the croquettes, then cook for 4 minutes and turn another third. Cook them for 4 minutes more. 4. Garnish the croquettes with the remaining dill after cooking, and serve warm.

Per Serving: Calories 213; Fat 10.3g; Sodium 401mg; Carbs 1.72g; Fibre 0.5g; Sugar 0.36g; Protein 28.04g

Tuna on Tomatoes

Prep Time: 10 minutes | **Cook Time:** 4 minutes | **Serves:** 2

1 (150g) can tuna in water, drained
55g mayonnaise
2 teaspoons yellow mustard
1 tablespoon minced dill pickle
1 tablespoon minced celery
1 tablespoon peeled and minced yellow onion
⅛ teaspoon salt
⅛ teaspoon freshly ground black pepper
4 thick slices large beef tomato
1 small avocado, peeled, pitted, and cut into 8 slices
50g grated mild Cheddar cheese

1. Combine tuna, mayonnaise, mustard, pickles, celery, onion, salt, and pepper in a medium bowl. 2. Preheat the air fryer to 175°C. Line the air fryer basket with parchment paper. 3. Place the tomato slices on the parchment paper in single layer, place two avocado slices on each tomato slice, distribute tuna salad over avocado slices, and top them evenly with cheese. 4. Place stacks in the air fryer basket, and cook for 4 minutes until cheese starts to brown. 5. Serve warm.

Per Serving: Calories 402; Fat 28.32g; Sodium 977mg; Carbs 16.38g; Fibre 8.5g; Sugar 4.02g; Protein 25.19g

Smoked Salmon with Baked Avocados

Prep Time: 10 minutes | **Cook Time:** 8 minutes | **Serves:** 2

60ml apple cider vinegar
1 teaspoon granulated sweetener
15g peeled and sliced red onion
50g cream cheese, room temperature
1 tablespoon capers, drained
2 large avocados, peeled, halved, and pitted
100g smoked salmon
2 medium cherry tomatoes, halved

1. Heat apple cider vinegar and sweetener in a small saucepan over high heat for 4 minutes until boiling; add onion, and then remove saucepan from heat. Let sit. Drain when ready to use onions. 2. Combine cream cheese and capers in a small bowl, cover the bowl and refrigerate them until ready to use. 3. Preheat the air fryer to 175°C. 4. Place avocado halves in the air fryer basket with cut sides up, and cook them in the air fryer for 4 minutes. 5. Transfer avocados to two medium plates and garnish with cream cheese mixture, smoked salmon, pickled onions, and tomato halves. Enjoy.

Per Serving: Calories 503; Fat 40.62g; Sodium 662mg; Carbs 23.96g; Fibre 14.1g; Sugar 6.38g; Protein 17.49g

Salmon Cakes with Special Sauce

Prep Time: 10 minutes | **Cook Time:** 20 minutes | **Serves:** 4

For Lemon Caper Sauce
60g sour cream
2 tablespoons mayonnaise
2 cloves garlic, peeled and minced
¼ teaspoon caper juice
2 teaspoons lemon juice

For Salmon Patties

1 (370g) can salmon, drained

110g mayonnaise

2 teaspoons lemon zest

1 large egg

2 tablespoons seeded and finely minced red pepper

50g almond meal

⅛ teaspoon salt

2 tablespoons capers, drained

1. To make the lemon caper sauce: Combine sour cream, mayonnaise, garlic, caper juice, and lemon juice in a small bowl; cover the bowl and refrigerate the mixture until ready to use. 2. To make salmon patties: Preheat air fryer to 200°C. Lightly grease the air fryer basket with olive oil. 3. Combine salmon, mayonnaise, lemon zest, egg, pepper, almond meal, and salt in a medium bowl, and form the mixture into eight patties. 4. Place four patties in the air fryer basket, and cook them for 10 minutes, gently flipping them halfway through. You can cook the patties in 2 batches. 5. Transfer cooked patties to a large serving dish, and let them rest for 5 minutes, then drizzle with lemon caper sauce and garnish with capers. Enjoy.

Per Serving: Calories 333; Fat 22.31g; Sodium 953mg; Carbs 5.52g; Fibre 1g; Sugar 1.75g; Protein 26.57g

Lemon Jumbo Sea Scallops

Prep Time: 5 minutes | **Cook Time:** 8 minutes | **Serves:** 2

2 tablespoons butter, melted

1 tablespoon fresh lemon juice

454g (about 10) jumbo sea scallops

1. Preheat the air fryer to 200°C. 2. Combine the butter and lemon juice in a small bowl, then coat the scallops with mixture on all sides. 3. Place the scallops in air fryer basket, cook them for 4 minutes, flipping them halfway through. 4. When the time is up, brush the tops of each scallop with butter mixture, and cook for 2 minutes, then flip them again and cook for 2 minutes more. 5. Serve warm.

Per Serving: Calories 228; Fat 8.84g; Sodium 894mg; Carbs 7.74g; Fibre 0g; Sugar 0.19g; Protein 27.84g

Prep Day Chicken Breasts

Prep Time: 5 minutes | **Cook Time:** 9 minutes | **Serves:** 4
2 teaspoons of olive oil
4 x115g boneless, skinless chicken breasts
½ teaspoon of salt
¼ teaspoon of ground black pepper

1. Preheat the air fryer to 175°C. 2. Lightly brush the chicken breasts with oil, and season them with salt and pepper. 3. Add the chicken breasts to the air fryer basket and cook them for 9 minutes, until they have an internal temperature of at least 75°C, flipping them halfway through. 4. Transfer the chicken to a large serving plate and let rest for 5 minutes. Chop and refrigerate, covered up, for up to 7 days.
Per Serving: Calories 215; Fat 12.75g; Sodium 362mg; Carbs 0.11g; Fibre 0g; Sugar 0g; Protein 23.66g

Salsa Verde Chicken

Prep Time: 5 minutes | **Cook Time:** 30 minutes | **Serves:** 4
4 x 115g boneless, skinless chicken thighs
215g of salsa Verde

1. Preheat the air fryer to 175°C for 3 minutes. 2. Place the chicken thighs in a suitable cake barrel and cover them with the salsa verde. 3. Place the pan in the air fryer basket and cook the chicken thighs for 30 minutes, until they have an internal temperature of at least 75°C. 4. Let the chicken thighs rest for 5 minutes before serving.
Per Serving: Calories 269; Fat 18.95g; Sodium550mg; Carbs 4.65g; Fibre 1.2g; Sugar 2.56g; Protein 19.73g

Chicken Bulgogi with Rice

Prep Time: 15 minutes | **Cook Time:** 11 minutes | **Serves:** 4
For Quick Pickled Carrots
2 medium carrots, grated
60ml of rice vinegar
2 teaspoons of granulated sugar
⅛ teaspoon of salt
For Chicken and Bulgogi Sauce
2 tablespoons of tamari
2 teaspoons of sesame oil
1 tablespoon of light brown sugar
1 tablespoon of rice vinegar
1 tablespoon of lime juice
2 cloves of garlic, peeled and minced
2 teaspoons of minced fresh ginger
3 spring onions, sliced, whites and greens separated
6 x 115g boneless, skinless chicken thighs, cut into 25mm cubes
700g of cooked white rice
2 teaspoons of sesame seeds

1. To make Quick Pickled Carrots, combine all the Quick Pickled Carrots ingredients in a medium bowl, cover the bowl, and refrigerate the carrots until ready to use. 2. To make the Chicken and Bulgogi Sauce, whisk the tamari, sesame oil, brown sugar, rice vinegar, lime juice, garlic, ginger, and whites of the spring onions in a large bowl, add chicken thighs, and let them marinate for 10 minutes. 3. Preheat the air fryer at 175°C for 3 minutes. 4. Place the marinated chicken thighs in the air fryer basket. Reserve the remaining marinade. 5. Cook the chicken thighs for 11 minutes, until they have an internal temperature of 75°C, pouring the remaining marinade over them halfway through. 6. Place the chicken thighs over rice on serving plates, garnish with the greens of the spring onions and the sesame seeds, and then serve with the Quick Pickled Carrots on the side.
Per Serving: Calories 336; Fat 8.35g; Sodium 630mg; Carbs 52.87g; Fibre 2.1g; Sugar 4.79g; Protein 10.78g

Breaded Drumettes

Prep Time: 10 minutes | **Cook Time:** 20 minutes | **Serves:** 2
455g of chicken drumettes
240g of buttermilk

90g of gluten-free breadcrumbs
½ teaspoon of smoked paprika
½ teaspoon of garlic powder
½ teaspoon of salt

1. Toss the drumettes with buttermilk in a bowl, then cover the bowl and refrigerate the drumettes overnight. 2. Preheat the air fryer at 175°C for 3 minutes. Lightly grease the air fryer basket with cooking oil. 3. Combine the breadcrumbs, paprika, garlic powder, and salt in a shallow dish. Shake excess buttermilk off the drumettes and dredge in the breadcrumb mixture. 4. Add the chicken to the air fryer basket and cook them for 12 minutes. 5. When the time is up, increase the cooking temperature to 200°C, flip the drumettes and resume cooking them for 8 minutes, until they have an internal temperature of at least 75°C, turning them over once more halfway through. 6. Let the dish cool for 5 minutes before serving.
Per Serving: Calories 340; Fat 7.72g; Sodium 1631mg; Carbs 13.28g; Fibre 0.6g; Sugar 6.69g; Protein 51.51g

Flavourful Chicken Legs

Prep Time: 10 minutes | **Cook Time:** 36 minutes | **Serves:** 4

280g of plain Greek yoghurt
1 tablespoon of Dijon mustard
1 teaspoon of smoked paprika
1 teaspoon of garlic powder
1 teaspoon of dried oregano
1 teaspoon of dried thyme
⅛ teaspoon of ground nutmeg
1 teaspoon of salt
1 teaspoon of ground black pepper
6 x 115g chicken legs 3 tablespoons of butter, melted

1.Toss the chicken legs with yoghurt, Dijon mustard, smoked paprika, garlic powder, dried oregano, dried thyme, nutmeg, salt, and pepper in a bowl, then cover the bowl, and refrigerate them for 60 minutes to overnight. 2. Preheat the air fryer at 190°C for 3 minutes. Lightly grease the air fryer basket with cooking oil. 3. Shake excess marinade from the chicken. Add the chicken legs to the air fryer basket and cook them for 10 minutes. 4. When the time is up, lightly brush them with melted butter, flip them and brush the other side with butter, and then resume cooking them for 8 minutes more until they have an internal temperature of at least 75°C. 5. You can cook the chicken legs in 2 batches. 6. Let the chicken legs stand for 5 minutes before serving.
Per Serving: Calories 399; Fat 22.25g; Sodium 1503mg; Carbs 4.68g; Fibre 0.8g; Sugar 2.99g; Protein 44.16g

Greek Chicken Salad

Prep Time: 10 minutes | **Cook Time:** 10 minutes | **Serves:** 2

For Dressing
280g of plain Greek yoghurt
½ medium English cucumber, peeled and small-diced
1 teaspoon of chopped fresh dill
1 teaspoon of chopped fresh mint
½ teaspoon of salt
1 teaspoon of lemon juice
2 cloves of garlic, peeled and minced
For Chicken
455g of boneless, skinless chicken cutlets, cut into ″10mm-thick strips
½ teaspoon of salt
¼ teaspoon of ground black pepper
For Salad
45g of mixed greens
35g of diced peeled red onion
10 kalamata olives, pitted and halved
1 large Roma tomato, diced
20g of feta cheese crumbles

1. Preheat the air fryer at 175°C for 3 minutes. Lightly grease the air fryer basket with cooking oil. 2. To make the dressing, mix all the dressing ingredients in a small bowl, cover the bowl, and refrigerate for up to 7 days. 3. To prepare the chicken, place the chicken strips in a medium bowl and season them with salt and pepper. 4. Add the chicken strips to the air fryer basket and cook them for 10 minutes, until they have an internal temperature of at least 75°C, gently

tossing them halfway through. 5. To make the salad, add the mixed greens to two medium salad bowls, garnish with onions, olives, tomatoes, and feta cheese. Top the salad with the chicken and drizzle with dressing. Enjoy.

Per Serving: Calories 515; Fat 28.6g; Sodium 1816mg; Carbs 17.35g; Fibre 4.8g; Sugar 10.22g; Protein 49.7g

Barbecue Chicken Legs

Prep Time: 10 minutes | **Cook Time:** 36 minutes | **Serves:** 4

4 spring onions, sliced, whites and greens separated
60ml of tamari
2 tablespoons sesame oil
85g of honey
2 tablespoons of gochujang
4 cloves of garlic, peeled and minced
½ teaspoon of ground ginger
1 teaspoon of salt
½ teaspoon of ground white pepper
6 x 115g chicken legs

1. Mince the whites of the spring onions. Set the greens aside. 2. Combine the tamari, sesame oil, honey, gochujang, garlic, ginger, salt, pepper, and the minced whites of the spring onions in a medium bowl. Reserve 60ml of the marinade. 3. Add the chicken legs to the tamari mixture bowl, then cover the bowl and refrigerate for 30 minutes. 4. Preheat the air fryer at 175°C for 3 minutes. Lightly grease the air fryer basket with cooking oil. 5. Add the chicken legs to the air fryer basket and cook for 10 minutes. 6. Flip the chicken legs and increase the cooking temperature to 200°C, then resume cooking them for 8 minutes, until they have an internal temperature of at least 75°C. 7. You can cook the chicken legs in 2 batches. 8. Let the chicken legs stand for 5 minutes after cooking, then toss them with the remaining sauce and garnish with the sliced greens from the spring onions and enjoy.

Per Serving: Calories 354; Fat 14.08g; Sodium 1818mg; Carbs 21.86g; Fibre 0.9g; Sugar 18.74g; Protein 35.28g

Cream Chicken Patties

Prep Time: 10 minutes | **Cook Time:** 26 minutes | **Serves:** 4

25g of crumbled blue cheese
60ml of sour cream
⅛ teaspoon of salt
3 tablespoons of buffalo wing sauce, divided
455g of ground chicken
2 tablespoons of finely grated carrot
2 tablespoons of finely diced celery
1 large egg white

1. Combine the blue cheese, sour cream, salt, and 1 tablespoon of the buffalo wing sauce in a small bowl, cover the bowl, and refrigerate until you are ready to serve the patties. 2. Preheat the air fryer at 175°C for 3 minutes. Lightly grease the air fryer basket with cooking oil. 3. Mix the chicken, carrot, celery, egg white and the remaining buffalo sauce in a large bowl, then make the mixture into 4 patties, making a slight indentation in middle of each. 4. Place the patties in the air fryer basket, and cook them for 13 minutes, flipping them halfway through. You can cook then patties in batches. 5. Serve the patties with the blue cheese sauce.

Per Serving: Calories 222; Fat 6.03g; Sodium 430mg; Carbs 11.86g; Fibre 1.7g; Sugar 7.03g; Protein 29.03g

Chicken Satay Kebabs

Prep Time: 10 minutes | **Cook Time:** 24 minutes | **Serves:** 4

For Peanut Sauce
60g of creamy peanut butter
1 tablespoon of pure maple syrup
1 tablespoon of tamari
1 tablespoon of lime juice
¼ teaspoon of sriracha
2 teaspoons of finely chopped peeled yellow onion
¼ teaspoon of minced fresh ginger
1 clove of garlic, peeled and minced
2 tablespoons of water
For Marinade
235ml of coconut milk
1 tablespoon of peanut Sauce

1 teaspoon of sriracha sauce
1 tablespoon of chopped fresh coriander
2x230g boneless, skinless chicken breasts, cut into 8 (25mm-thick) strips

1. To make the peanut sauce, mix all the sauce ingredients in a small bowl, and set aside. Reserve 1 tablespoon. 2. To make the marinade, combine the reserved peanut sauce, coconut milk, sriracha sauce, and coriander in a medium bowl. Toss in the chicken strips, then cover the bowl and refrigerate for 15 minutes. 3. Preheat the air fryer at 175°C for 3 minutes. 4. Skewer the chicken strips and place them on a kebab rack. 5. Place the kebab rack in the air fryer basket and cook them for 12 minutes. You can cook them in batches. 6. Serve warm with the peanut sauce on the side.

Per Serving: Calories 424; Fat 22.84g; Sodium 484mg; Carbs 23.96g; Fibre 2.8g; Sugar 15.5g; Protein 32.52g

Curry Chicken Salad

Prep Time: 10 minutes | **Cook Time:** 18 minutes | **Serves:** 2

2 x 230g boneless, skinless chicken breasts 1 teaspoon of salt
¼ teaspoon of ground black pepper
165g of mayonnaise
1 tablespoon of fresh lime juice
1 teaspoon of curry powder
75g of chopped golden raisins
1 small Granny Smith apple, peeled, cored, and grated
1 medium spring onion, minced
2 tablespoons of chopped pecans

1. Preheat the air fryer at 175°C for 3 minutes. Lightly grease the air fryer basket with cooking oil. 2. Season the chicken breasts with salt and pepper. 3. Add the chicken breasts to the air fryer basket and cook them for 9 minutes, until they have an internal temperature of at least 75°C, shaking the basket gently and flipping the chicken breast halfway through. You can cook them in batches. 4. Let the chicken breasts stand for 7 minutes, then chop them and toss them in

a large bowl with the remaining ingredients, then cover the bowl and refrigerate them until ready to eat.

Per Serving: Calories 526; Fat 23.64g; Sodium 1347mg; Carbs 54.81g; Fibre 4.9g; Sugar 32.5g; Protein 27.84g

Chicken Club Sandwiches

Prep Time: 10 minutes | **Cook Time:** 36 minutes | **Serves:** 4

240ml buttermilk
1 large egg
100g gluten-free plain bread crumbs
1 teaspoon garlic powder
1 teaspoon salt
1 teaspoon ground black pepper
4 chicken breasts (about 750g)
3 tablespoons butter, melted
4 gluten-free burger buns
4 tablespoons mayonnaise
4 teaspoons yellow mustard
4 pieces iceberg lettuce
4 slices cooked bacon
8 thin slices vine-ripe tomato

1. Preheat the air fryer at 175°C for 3 minutes. Lightly grease the air fryer basket with cooking oil. 2. Beat the egg with buttermilk in a medium bowl. 3. Combine bread crumbs, garlic powder, salt, and black pepper in a shallow dish. 4. Dip chicken in buttermilk mixture, then dredge in bread crumb mixture. Shake off any excess crumb mixture. 5. Add the chicken cutlets to air fryer basket, and cook them for 10 minutes. 6. When the time is up, lightly brush the chicken with melted butter, and increase the cooking temperature to 200°C, and then cook them for 8 minutes more until they have an internal temperature of at least 75°C. 7. You can cook the chicken in batches. 8. Allow the cooked chicken breasts to cool for 5 minutes after cooking. 8. Assemble sandwiches by spreading mayonnaise on top buns and mustard on bottom buns. Place chicken on bottom buns. Top with lettuce, bacon, and tomatoes. Serve warm.

Per Serving: Calories 622; Fat 23.16g; Sodium 1546mg; Carbs 38.26g; Fibre 4g; Sugar 8.02g; Protein 63.48g

Chicken Cobb Salad

Prep Time: 10 minutes | **Cook Time:** 18 minutes | **Serves:** 4

For Chicken
1 large egg
1 tablespoon honey
1 tablespoon Dijon mustard
½ teaspoon apple cider vinegar
2 (100g) boneless, skinless chicken breasts (approximately 225g), cut into 2.5cm cubes
80g plain gluten-free bread crumbs
½ teaspoon salt
½ teaspoon ground black pepper

For Salad
170g chopped iceberg lettuce
120ml ranch dressing
½ medium avocado, peeled, pitted, and diced
1 medium beef tomato, diced
1 large hard-boiled egg, diced
4 slices cooked bacon, crumbled
15g diced peeled red onion

1. Preheat air fryer at 175°C for 3 minutes. Lightly grease the air fryer basket with cooking oil. 2. Whisk the egg, honey, Dijon mustard, and vinegar in a medium bowl, then toss in chicken cubes. 3. Combine bread crumbs, salt, and pepper in a shallow dish. Shake excess marinade off chicken and dredge in bread crumb mixture. 4. Add the chicken cubes to air fryer basket, and cook them for 9 minutes until they have an internal temperature of at least 75°C, shaking the basket gently halfway through. 5. You can cook the chicken cubes in batches. 6. Transfer the cooked chicken cubes to a large plate after cooking. 7. To make salad, toss the lettuce and ranch dressing in two serving bowls. Top with avocado, tomato, egg, bacon, onion, and chicken. Serve.
Per Serving: Calories 322; Fat 24.16g; Sodium 770mg; Carbs 16.29g; Fibre 3.4g; Sugar 9.01g; Protein 12.18g

Delicious Chicken Avocado Paninis

Prep Time: 10 minutes | **Cook Time:** 12 minutes | **Serves:** 2
2 tablespoons mayonnaise
4 teaspoons yellow mustard
4 slices gluten-free sandwich bread
100g thinly sliced deli chicken
100g thinly sliced provolone cheese
1 small avocado, peeled, pitted, and thinly sliced
1 medium tomato, thinly sliced
¼ teaspoon salt
¼ teaspoon ground black pepper
2 tablespoons butter, melted

1. Preheat the air fryer at 175°C for 3 minutes. 2. Spread mayonnaise and mustard on inside of each bread slice. 3. Evenly distribute chicken, provolone, avocado, and tomato on slices to build sandwiches. Sprinkle tomato with salt and pepper, then close sandwiches. 4. Brush top and bottom of each sandwich lightly with melted butter. Place the sandwich in the air fryer basket, and cook for 6 minutes, flipping halfway through. 5. Do the same with the remaining sandwich. 6. Transfer sandwiches to serving plates and press gently with back of a skillet. Serve warm.
Per Serving: Calories 760; Fat 47.19g; Sodium 1924mg; Carbs 48.84g; Fibre 13.5g; Sugar 7.35g; Protein 26.49g

Breaded Chicken Strips

Prep Time: 10 minutes | **Cook Time:** 10 minutes | **Serves:** 2
454g boneless, skinless chicken breast, cut into 0.6cm thick strips
235g ketchup
55g gluten-free bread crumbs
80g polenta

1. Coat the chicken strips with ketchup in a medium bowl. 2. Preheat the air fryer at 175°C for 3 minutes. Lightly grease the air fryer basket with cooking oil. 3. Combine bread crumbs and polenta in a shallow dish.

Shake off excess ketchup from chicken strips and dredge in bread crumb mixture. Shake off any excess. 4. Add chicken strips to air fryer basket, and cook for 4 minutes. 5. Toss chicken gently. Cook an additional 4 minutes. 6. Toss chicken gently once more. Cook 2 more minutes to ensure internal temperature is at least 75°C. 7. Serve warm.

Per Serving: Calories 537; Fat 4.8g; Sodium 1250mg; Carbs 68.39g; Fibre 2.1g; Sugar 26.65g; Protein 55.16g

Mustard Chicken Bites

Prep Time: 10 minutes | **Cook Time:** 10 minutes | **Serves:** 4

2 tablespoons horseradish mustard
1 tablespoon olive oil
2 (200g) boneless, skinless chicken breasts cut into 2.5cm cubes

1. Whisk the horseradish mustard and olive oil in a medium bowl; add chicken cubes and toss them well, the cover the bowl and refrigerate them for 30 minutes up to overnight. 2. Preheat the air fryer at 175°C for 3 minutes. Lightly grease the air fryer basket with cooking oil. 3. Add chicken to air fryer basket, and cook them for 4 minutes. 4. Toss chicken gently, and cook them for an additional 5 minutes until they have an internal temperature of at least 75°C. 5. Serve warm.

Per Serving: Calories 116; Fat 5.66g; Sodium 272mg; Carbs 0.45g; Fibre 0.3g; Sugar 0.07g; Protein 16.19g

Chicken Parmesan Pizzadillas

Prep Time: 10 minutes | **Cook Time:** 12 minutes | **Serves:** 4

280g cooked boneless, skinless chicken, shredded
½ teaspoon salt
1 teaspoon garlic powder
3 tablespoons butter, melted
8 (15cm) gluten-free flour tortillas
265g marinara sauce
115g grated mozzarella cheese
115g grated provolone cheese
8 large fresh basil leaves, julienned

1. Preheat the air fryer to 175°C for 3 minutes. 2. Toss the chicken with salt and garlic powder in a medium bowl. 3. Lightly brush the melted butter on one side of a tortilla. Place tortilla in the air fryer basket with butter-side down. 4. Spread 65 g marinara sauce on tortilla. Layer ¼ of chicken, ¼ of mozzarella, 1/4 of provolone, and ¼ basil leaves on top. Top with second tortilla. Lightly butter the top tortilla. 5. Cook pizzadilla in the air fryer for 3 minutes. Set aside and do the same with the remaining ingredients (yields four pizzadillas total). 6. Slice each pizzadilla into six sections. Serve warm.

Per Serving: Calories 652; Fat 27.82g; Sodium 2080mg; Carbs 54.94g; Fibre 4.1g; Sugar 5.8g; Protein 45.49g

Lemony Chicken Meatballs

Prep Time: 10 minutes | **Cook Time:** 10 minutes | **Serves:** 6

454g chicken mince
1 large egg
80g gluten-free bread crumbs
15g finely diced peeled yellow onion
1 teaspoon Italian seasoning
2 teaspoons lemon zest
1 teaspoon salt
½ teaspoon ground black pepper
15g chopped fresh parsley

1. Preheat air fryer at 175°C for 3 minutes. 2. Toss the chicken mince with egg, bread crumbs, onion, Italian seasoning, lemon zest, salt, and pepper in a large bowl, then make the mixture into eighteen meatballs, about 2 tablespoons each. 3. Add nine meatballs to the air fryer basket, and cook them for 6 minutes, then flip them and cook for an additional 2 minutes. 4. You can cook the meatballs in batches. 5. Transfer the meatballs to the serving bowl or plate, garnish with chopped parsley, and enjoy.

Per Serving: Calories 233; Fat 12.93g; Sodium 588mg; Carbs 10.94g; Fibre 0.9g; Sugar 1.19g; Protein 17.09g

Jalapeño Chicken Meatballs

Prep Time: 10 minutes | **Cook Time:** 10 minutes | **Serves:** 4

For Quick Pickled Jalapeños
2 medium jalapeños, seeded and small-diced
2 tablespoons white wine vinegar
½ teaspoon granulated sugar
⅛ teaspoon salt

For Cheese Centre
1 tablespoon cream cheese
2 tablespoons shredded Cheddar cheese
1 teaspoon quick pickled jalapeños

For Chicken Meatballs
340g chicken mince
Remaining pickled jalapeños
¼ teaspoon smoked paprika
¼ teaspoon salt

For Breading
100g gluten-free bread crumbs
¼ teaspoon salt
1 tablespoon butter, melted

1. To make the pickled jalapeños, combine diced jalapeños, white wine vinegar, sugar, and salt in a small bowl, then refrigerate them for 15 minutes. 2. To make cheese centre, mix the cream cheese, Cheddar cheese, and 1 teaspoon of refrigerated pickled jalapeños in another small bowl, then make the mixture into eight balls. 3. To make the chicken meatballs, combine the chicken mince, smoked paprika, salt, and the remaining pickled jalapeños in a medium bowl, then form the mixture into eight meatballs. 4. Form a hole in one chicken meatball. Press a cheese ball into hole and form chicken around cheese ball, sealing cheese ball in meatball. Do the same with the remaining chicken meatballs and cheese balls. 5. Preheat the air fryer at 175°C for 3 minutes. Lightly grease the air fryer basket with cooking oil. 6. To make breading, mix the bread crumbs and salt in a shallow dish. Roll stuffed meatballs in bread crumbs. 7. Add meatballs to air fryer basket lightly, and cook them for 10 minutes, flipping and brushing them with melted butter halfway through. 8. Serve warm.

Per Serving: Calories 287; Fat 12.02g; Sodium 1222mg; Carbs 24.96g; Fibre 3.2g; Sugar 4.97g; Protein 20.07g

Chicken Quesadillas

Prep Time: 10 minutes | **Cook Time:** 12 minutes | **Serves:** 4

170g sour cream
2 teaspoons chili powder
280g cooked boneless, skinless chicken breast, shredded
1 (175g) can diced green chilies, including juice
½ teaspoon salt
3 tablespoons butter, melted
8 (15cm) gluten-free flour tortillas
225g grated Mexican cheese blend

1. Combine sour cream and chili powder in a small bowl, then cover the bowl, and refrigerate them until ready to serve. 2. Combine chicken, green chilies, and salt in a medium bowl. 3. Preheat the air fryer to 175°C. 4. Lightly brush melted butter on one side of a tortilla. Place tortilla in the air fryer basket with the butter-side down. Layer one-quarter of chicken mixture on tortilla, followed by one-quarter of cheese. Top with second tortilla. Lightly butter top of second tortilla. 5. Cook the quesadilla for 3 minutes. You can cook them in batches. 6. Slice each quesadilla into six sections. Serve warm with sour cream mixture on the side for dipping.

Per Serving: Calories 482; Fat 25.42g; Sodium 784mg; Carbs 30.75g; Fibre 4g; Sugar 1g; Protein 33.49g

Cheese Spaghetti Pie

Prep Time: 15 minutes | **Cook Time:** 22 minutes | **Serves:** 4

For Ricotta Cheese Layer
167g ricotta cheese
1 tablespoon grated Parmesan cheese
½ teaspoon salt

For Spaghetti Crust
2 tablespoons butter, melted
1 large egg
45g grated Parmesan cheese

¼ teaspoon salt
178g dry gluten-free spaghetti, cooked according to instructions
For Toppings
2 teaspoons olive oil
17g diced peeled onion
52g diced seeded green pepper
114g minced chicken
225g marinara sauce
112g grated mozzarella cheese

1. To make the ricotta cheese layer, combine all the ricotta cheese layer ingredients in a small bowl. 2. To make the spaghetti crust, mix the butter, egg, Parmesan, and salt in a large bowl; stir in the drained, cooled cooked spaghetti. Set aside. 3. To make the toppings, heat the olive oil in a medium pan, over a medium heat for 30 seconds; add onion and pepper. Cook for 3 minutes until the onions are translucent then add the minced chicken. Stir-fry for 5 minutes until no longer pink. 4. Preheat the air fryer at 350°F/ 175°C for 3 minutes. Lightly grease the air fryer basket with cooking oil. 5. Gently press the spaghetti mixture into a 7" spring-form tin, spread the ricotta mixture evenly on top. Top with the toppings mixture, followed by the marinara sauce. 6. Place spring-form tin in the air fryer basket and cook for 10 minutes. 7. Spread mozzarella cheese evenly on top and cook for an additional 4 minutes. 8. Transfer the tin onto a cutting board and let rest for 20 minutes. Once set, release the sides of the spring-form tin. Slice and serve pie.
Per Serving: Calories 355; Fat 19.34g; Sodium 1321mg; Carbs 22.5g; Fiber 2.4g; Sugar 3.77g; Protein 23.46g

Buttermilk Cornish Hen

Prep Time: 10 minutes | **Cook Time:** 28 minutes | **Serves:** 2
484g buttermilk (or milk with vinegar or lemon juice added)
1 teaspoon salt
1 teaspoon ground black pepper
½ teaspoon ground celery seed
1 Cornish hen (Poussin) (approximately 900g)
1 tablespoon olive oil
½ medium lime, halved
2 garlic cloves, peeled and halved
2 sprigs fresh rosemary

1. Toss the Cornish hen with buttermilk, salt, pepper, and celery seed in a bowl, then cover the bowl and put in the fridge for 2 hours or up to overnight. 2. Preheat the air fryer at 350°F/ 175°C for 3 minutes. 3. Pat hen dry with kitchen towel. Drizzle oil over the top and inside the hen. Stuff lime, garlic, and rosemary sprigs into the hen's cavity. 4. Place the hen in the air fryer basket and cook for 10 minutes. Turn the hen and cook for a further 10 minutes. Then, turn the hen once more and cook for an additional 8 minutes until it reaches the internal temperature of at least 165°F/ 75°C. 5. Transfer the hen to a cutting board and let it rest for 5 minutes, then discard lime, garlic cloves, and rosemary. 6. Cut down spine of hen and serve warm.
Per Serving: Calories 312; Fat 13.2g; Sodium 1712mg; Carbs 15.14g; Fiber 0.8g; Sugar 11.96g; Protein 32.69g

Savory Wings

Prep Time: 5 minutes | **Cook Time:** 25 minutes | **Serves:** 4
900g bone-in chicken wings, separated at joints
1 teaspoon salt
½ teaspoon ground black pepper

1. Season the chicken wings with salt and pepper, then place in the air fryer basket in a single layer. 2. Cook the chicken wings at 400°F/ 200°C for 25 minutes until they are golden brown and have an internal temperature of at least 165°F/ 75°C, shaking the basket every 7 minutes during cooking. 3. Serve warm.
Per Serving: Calories 287; Fat 8.04g; Sodium 765mg; Carbs 0.24g; Fiber 0.1g; Sugar 0g; Protein 49.87g

Garlicky Wings

Prep Time: 5 minutes | **Cook Time:** 25 minutes | **Serves:** 4

900g bone-in chicken wings, separated at joints
½ teaspoon salt
½ teaspoon ground black pepper
½ teaspoon onion powder
½ teaspoon garlic powder
1 teaspoon dried dill

1. Toss the chicken wings with salt, pepper, onion powder, garlic powder, and dill in a large bowl until evenly coated. 2. Place the chicken wings in the air fryer basket in a single layer. 3. Cook the wings at 400°F/ 200°C for 25 minutes until they have an internal temperature of at least 165°F/ 75°C, shaking the basket every 7 minutes during cooking. 4. Serve warm.

Per Serving: Calories 291; Fat 8.12g; Sodium 475mg; Carbs 1.06g; Fiber 0.3g; Sugar 0.03g; Protein 50.05g

Fajita Chicken Thigh Meatballs

Prep Time: 10 minutes | **Cook Time:** 20 minutes | **Serves:** 6

454g minced chicken thighs
½ medium green pepper, seeded and finely chopped
¼ medium onion, peeled and finely chopped
112g shredded pepper jack cheese
1 (28g) packet gluten-free fajita seasoning

1. Combine all ingredients in a large bowl, form the mixture into eighteen 2" balls. 2. Place the balls in the air fryer basket in a single layer. 3. Cook the meatballs at 350°F/ 175°C for 20 minutes, turning them halfway through cooking. 4. When there is 5 minutes left, increase the temperature to 400°F/ 200°C to give the balls a dark golden-brown color, shaking the basket once more when there is 2 minutes left. 5. Serve warm.

Per Serving: Calories 221; Fat 15.09g; Sodium 333mg; Carbs 2.7g; Fiber 0.5g; Sugar 0.75g; Protein 15.44g

Pesto Chicken Pizzas

Prep Time: 10 minutes | **Cook Time:** 12 minutes | **Serves:** 4

454g minced chicken thighs
¼ teaspoon salt
⅛ teaspoon ground black pepper
56g basil pesto
111g shredded mozzarella cheese
4 cherry tomatoes, sliced

1. Line the air fryer basket with baking paper. 2. Mix the minced chicken with the salt and pepper in a large bowl. Divide mixture into four equal quarters. 3. Wet your hands with water, to prevent sticking, then press each quarter into a 6" circle and put on a piece of ungreased baking paper. 4. Place each chicken crust in the air fryer basket, working in batches if needed. 5. Cook the crusts at 350°F/ 175°C for 10 minutes, turning them halfway through cooking. 6. When the time is up, spread 1 tablespoon pesto across the top of each crust, then sprinkle with ¼ of the mozzarella and top with 1 sliced tomato, then resume cooking them for 2 minutes until the cheese is melted and brown. 7. Serve warm.

Per Serving: Calories 307; Fat 19.03g; Sodium 452mg; Carbs 4.92g; Fiber 1.6g; Sugar 2.82g; Protein 28.55g

Cheese Broccoli–Stuffed Chicken

Prep Time: 15 minutes | **Cook Time:** 20 minutes | **Serves:** 4

56g cream cheese, softened
71g chopped fresh broccoli, steamed
117g grated mature Cheddar cheese
4 (168g) boneless, skinless chicken breasts
2 tablespoons mayonnaise
¼ teaspoon salt
¼ teaspoon garlic powder
⅛ teaspoon ground black pepper

1. Combine cream cheese, broccoli, and Cheddar in a medium bowl. 2. Cut a 4" pocket into each chicken breast. Evenly divide the mixture between the chicken breasts, stuff the pocket of each chicken

breast with the mixture. 3. Spread ¼ tablespoon mayonnaise on each side of each chicken breast, then sprinkle both sides of the breasts with salt, garlic powder, and pepper. 4. Place the stuffed chicken breasts in the air fryer basket and cook them at 350°F/ 175°C for 20 minutes, turning them halfway through cooking. 5. When done, the chicken will be golden and have an internal temperature of at least 165°F/ 75°C. 6. Serve warm.
Per Serving: Calories 200; Fat 15.22g; Sodium 387mg; Carbs 1.52g; Fiber 0.4g; Sugar 0.64g; Protein 14.12g

Pickle-Brined Chicken

Prep Time: 1 hour 15 minutes | **Cook Time:** 20 minutes | **Serves:** 4
4 (113g) boneless, skinless chicken thighs
80ml dill pickle juice
1 large egg
56g plain pork rinds, crushed
½ teaspoon salt
¼ teaspoon ground black pepper

1. Place the chicken thighs in a large sealable bowl or bag and pour the pickle juice over them. Place sealed bowl or bag into the fridge and allow to marinate for at least 1 hour or up to overnight. 2. Beat the egg in a small bowl; place the pork rinds in another medium bowl. 3. Remove the chicken thighs from the marinade. Shake off any excess pickle juice and pat thighs dry with a kitchen towel. Sprinkle with salt and pepper. 4. Dip each thigh into the egg and gently shake off any excess. Press into the pork rinds to coat each side. 5. Place the thighs into an ungreased air fryer basket, and cook them at 400°F/ 200°C for 20 minutes, until they have an internal temperature of at least 165°F/ 75°C. 6. Serve warm.
Per Serving: Calories 159; Fat 10.38g; Sodium 685mg; Carbs 0.56g; Fiber 0.2g; Sugar 0.17g; Protein 15.02g

Spiced Chicken Thighs

Prep Time: 10 minutes | **Cook Time:** 25 minutes | **Serves:** 4

4 (113g) bone-in, skin-on chicken thighs
½ teaspoon salt
½ teaspoon garlic powder
2 teaspoons chilli powder
1 teaspoon paprika
1 teaspoon ground cumin
1 small lime, halved

1. Pat the chicken thighs dry and sprinkle with salt, garlic powder, chilli powder, paprika, and cumin. 2. Squeeze the juice from ½ a lime over the thighs, and then place the thighs in the air fryer basket. 3. Cook the thighs at 380°F/ 195°C for 25 minutes until they are crispy and browned with an internal temperature of at least 165°F/ 75°C, turning the thighs halfway through cooking. 4. Drizzle with remaining the lime juice and serve warm.
Per Serving: Calories 74; Fat 5.1g; Sodium 354mg; Carbs 2.5g; Fiber 0.8g; Sugar 0.36g; Protein 5.15g

Pork Rind Fried Chicken

Prep Time: 40 minutes | **Cook Time:** 20 minutes | **Serves:** 4
60ml buffalo sauce
4 (113g) boneless, skinless chicken breasts
½ teaspoon paprika
½ teaspoon garlic powder
¼ teaspoon ground black pepper
56g plain pork rinds, finely crushed

1. Toss the chicken breasts with buffalo sauce in a large sealable bag, then place the bag in the fridge to let them marinate for at least 30 minutes or up to overnight. 2. Remove the chicken from the marinade but do not shake any excess sauce off chicken. Sprinkle the thighs with paprika, garlic powder, and pepper on both sides. 3. Place pork rinds in a large bowl, and evenly coat each chicken breast on both sides. 4. Place the chicken in the air fryer basket. Cook them at 400°F/ 200°C for 20 minutes until they are golden and have an internal temperature of at least 165°F/ 75°C. Turning the chicken halfway through cooking. 5. Serve warm.

Per Serving: Calories 160; Fat 7.22g; Sodium 460mg; Carbs 8.01g; Fiber 0.3g; Sugar 6.13g; Protein 14.91g

Palatable Chipotle Drumsticks

Prep Time: 5 minutes | **Cook Time:** 25 minutes | **Serves:** 4

1 tablespoon tomato paste
½ teaspoon chipotle powder
¼ teaspoon apple cider vinegar
¼ teaspoon garlic powder
8 chicken drumsticks
½ teaspoon salt
⅛ teaspoon ground black pepper

1. Combine tomato paste, chipotle powder, vinegar, and garlic powder in a small bowl. 2. Sprinkle drumsticks with salt and pepper, then place into a large bowl and pour in tomato paste mixture. Toss or stir to evenly coat all drumsticks in mixture. 3. Place drumsticks in air fryer basket, and cook them at 200°C for 25 minutes until they are dark red and have an internal temperature of at least 75°C. 4. Serve warm.

Per Serving: Calories 423; Fat 23.94g; Sodium 569mg; Carbs 1.29g; Fibre 0.2g; Sugar 0.52g; Protein 47.22g

Parmesan Drumsticks

Prep Time: 5 minutes | **Cook Time:** 25 minutes | **Serves:** 4

8 (100g) chicken drumsticks
½ teaspoon salt
⅛ teaspoon ground black pepper
½ teaspoon garlic powder
2 tablespoons salted butter, melted
50g grated Parmesan cheese
1 tablespoon dried parsley

1. Sprinkle the drumsticks with salt, pepper, and garlic powder, and then transfer them to the air fryer basket. 2. Cook the drumsticks at 200°C for 25 minutes until they are golden and have an internal temperature of at least 75°C. 3. Transfer drumsticks to a large serving dish. Pour butter over drumsticks, and sprinkle with Parmesan and parsley. Serve warm.

Per Serving: Calories 151; Fat 11.86g; Sodium 548mg; Carbs 2.26g; Fibre 0.1g; Sugar 0.11g; Protein 8.86g

Pecan-Crusted Chicken

Prep Time: 10 minutes | **Cook Time:** 12 minutes | **Serves:** 4

2 tablespoons mayonnaise
1 teaspoon Dijon mustard
454g boneless, skinless chicken mini fillets
½ teaspoon salt
¼ teaspoon ground black pepper
55g chopped roasted pecans, finely ground

1. Whisk mayonnaise and mustard in a small bowl. 2. Brush the chicken mini fillets with the mayonnaise mixture on both sides, then sprinkle with salt and pepper. 3. Place pecans in a medium bowl, and press each fillet into pecans to coat each side. 4. Place tenders in air fryer basket in a single layer, and cook them at 190°C for 12 minutes until they are golden brown have an internal temperature of at least 75°C. 5. Turn the tenders halfway through. 6. Serve warm.

Per Serving: Calories 237; Fat 14.4g; Sodium 448mg; Carbs 2.28g; Fibre 1.4g; Sugar 0.71g; Protein 24.74g

Flavourful Chicken Tenders

Prep Time: 5 minutes | **Cook Time:** 12 minutes | **Serves:** 4

454g boneless, skinless chicken mini fillets
2 tablespoons coconut oil, melted
1 teaspoon paprika
½ teaspoon chili powder
½ teaspoon salt
¼ teaspoon ground black pepper
¼ teaspoon garlic powder
¼ teaspoon cayenne pepper

1. Toss the chicken tenders with coconut oil in a large bowl, then sprinkle each side of chicken with paprika, chili powder, salt, black pepper, garlic powder, and cayenne pepper. 2. Place chicken in the air fryer basket, and

cook them at 190°C for 12 minutes until they are dark brown and have an internal temperature of at least 75°C. 3. Serve warm.

Per Serving: Calories 189; Fat 10.01g; Sodium 387mg; Carbs 0.97g; Fibre 0.4g; Sugar 0.25g; Protein 23.29g

Bacon Chicken

Prep Time: 10 minutes | **Cook Time:** 65 minutes | **Serves:** 6

1 (1.8kg) whole chicken
2 tablespoons salted butter, softened
1 teaspoon dried thyme
½ teaspoon garlic powder
1 teaspoon salt
½ teaspoon ground black pepper
6 slices bacon

1. Pat chicken dry with a paper towel, then rub with butter on all sides. Sprinkle thyme, garlic powder, salt, and pepper over chicken. 2. Place chicken in air fryer basket with breast side up, lay strips of bacon over chicken and secure with toothpicks. 3. Cook them at 175°C for 65 minutes, removing and setting aside bacon and flipping chicken over halfway through cooking. 4. Chicken will be done when the skin is golden and crispy and the internal temperature is at least 75°C. 5. Serve warm with bacon.

Per Serving: Calories 217; Fat 8.32g; Sodium 601mg; Carbs 0.9g; Fibre 0.2g; Sugar 0.2g; Protein 33.01g

Cheese Ham Chicken

Prep Time: 15 minutes | **Cook Time:** 25 minutes | **Serves:** 4

4 (150g) boneless, skinless chicken breasts
4 (25g) slices Swiss cheese
4 (25g) slices ham
60g Dijon mustard
½ teaspoon salt
¼ teaspoon ground black pepper

1. Cut a 12.5cm long slit in the side of each chicken breast. Place a slice of Swiss and a slice of ham inside each slit. 2. Brush chicken breasts with mustard, then sprinkle with salt and pepper on both sides. 3. Place chicken in air fryer basket, and cook them at 190°C for 25 minutes, turning chicken halfway through cooking. 4. Chicken will be golden brown and have an internal temperature of at least 75°C when done. 5. Serve warm.

Per Serving: Calories 216; Fat 12.46g; Sodium 571mg; Carbs 7.63g; Fibre 1.2g; Sugar 3.19g; Protein 18.11g

Cheese Chicken Nuggets

Prep Time: 10 minutes | **Cook Time:** 15 minutes | **Serves:** 4

454g chicken thigh mince
55g shredded mozzarella cheese
1 large egg, whisked
½ teaspoon salt
¼ teaspoon dried oregano
¼ teaspoon garlic powder

1. Combine all ingredients in a large bowl, then make the mixture into twenty nugget shapes, about 2 tablespoons each. 2. Place nuggets in air fryer basket, and cook them at 190°C for 15 minutes, turning nuggets halfway through cooking. 3. You can cook them in batches. 4. Let the dish cool 5 minutes before serving.

Per Serving: Calories 289; Fat 20.03g; Sodium 505mg; Carbs 1.07g; Fibre 0.3g; Sugar 0.26g; Protein 24.82g

Ginger Chicken Thigh Pieces

Prep Time: 30 minutes | **Cook Time:** 12 minutes | **Serves:** 4

454g boneless, skinless chicken thighs, cut into 2.5cm pieces
60ml soy sauce
2 cloves garlic, peeled and finely minced
1 tablespoon minced ginger
¼ teaspoon salt

1. Place all ingredients in a large sealable bag, then seal the bag and place it in the refrigerator to let the chicken thighs marinate for at least 30 minutes up to overnight. 2. Remove the chicken thigh pieces from marinade and place in the air fryer basket. 3.

Cook the chicken thigh pieces at 190°C for 12 minutes until they are golden and have an internal temperature of at least 75°C, shaking the basket twice during cooking. 4.. Serve warm.

Per Serving: Calories 247; Fat 9.35g; Sodium 689mg; Carbs 28.42g; Fibre 2.1g; Sugar 9.19g; Protein 11.77g

Chipotle Chicken Wings

Prep Time: 5 minutes | **Cook Time:** 25 minutes | **Serves:** 6

900g bone-in chicken wings
½ teaspoon salt
¼ teaspoon ground black pepper
2 tablespoons mayonnaise
2 teaspoons chipotle powder
2 tablespoons lemon juice

1. Toss the chicken wings with salt and pepper in a large bowl, then place them in air fryer basket. 2. Cook the chicken wings at 200°C for 25 minutes until they are golden and have an internal temperature of at least 75°C, shaking the basket twice while cooking. 3. Whisk the mayonnaise, chipotle powder, and lemon juice in a small bowl. Place cooked wings into a large serving bowl and drizzle with aioli. Toss to coat, and then enjoy.

Per Serving: Calories 211; Fat 6.97g; Sodium 356mg; Carbs 1.21g; Fibre 0.2g; Sugar 0.22g; Protein 33.63g

Cajun Chicken Bites

Prep Time: 10 minutes | **Cook Time:** 12 minutes | **Serves:** 4

454g boneless, skinless chicken breasts, cut into 2.5cm cubes
120g heavy whipping cream
½ teaspoon salt
¼ teaspoon ground black pepper
25g grated parmesan
60g unflavoured whey protein powder
½ teaspoon Cajun seasoning

1. Coat the chicken cubes with cream in a medium bowl, then sprinkle with salt and pepper. 2. Mix the parmesan, protein powder, and Cajun seasoning in another large bowl. 3. Remove the chicken cubes from cream, shaking off any excess, and toss in dry mix until fully coated. 4. Place bites in air fryer basket, and cook them at 200°C for 12 minutes, shaking the basket twice during cooking. 5. Bites will be done when golden brown and have an internal temperature of at least 75°C. 6. Serve warm.

Per Serving: Calories 335; Fat 16.12g; Sodium 790mg; Carbs 26.61g; Fibre 2.6g; Sugar 7.31g; Protein 20.27g

Blue Cheese Beef Burgers

Prep Time: 10 minutes | **Cook Time:** 20 minutes | **Serves:** 4

Olive oil for spraying
455g of lean ground beef
40g of blue cheese, crumbled
1 teaspoon of Worcestershire sauce
½ teaspoon of freshly ground black pepper
½ teaspoon of hot sauce
½ teaspoon of minced garlic
¼ teaspoon of salt
4 wholewheat buns

1. Lightly spray the air fryer basket with olive oil. 2. Mix the beef, blue cheese, Worcestershire sauce, pepper, hot sauce, garlic, and salt in a large bowl, then divide the mixture into 4 patties. 3. Place the patties in the fryer basket in a single layer, leaving a little room between them for even cooking. 5. Air fry the patties at 180°C for 20 minutes, until the meat reaches an internal temperature of at least 70°C, flipping them halfway through cooking. 6. Place each patty on a bun and serve with low-calorie toppings, such as sliced tomatoes or onions. Enjoy.
Per Serving: Calories 295; Fat 12.39g; Sodium 568mg; Carbs 16.44g; Fibre 2.2g; Sugar 0.47g; Protein 30.7g

Stuffed Bell Peppers

Prep Time: 15 minutes | **Cook Time:** 20 minutes | **Serves:** 4

Olive oil
4 large red bell peppers
455g of lean ground beef
130g of diced onion
Salt
Freshly ground black pepper
250g of cooked brown rice
55g of shredded, reduced-fat Cheddar cheese
110g of tomato sauce
2 tablespoons of dill pickle relish
2 tablespoons of ketchup
1 tablespoon of Worcestershire sauce
1 tablespoon of mustard
10g of shredded lettuce
100g of diced tomatoes

1. Lightly spray the air fryer basket with olive oil. 2. Cut about 15mm off the tops of the peppers and remove any seeds from the insides. Set aside. 3. Cook the ground beef and onion in a large skillet over medium-high heat for 5 minutes until browned, then season them with salt and pepper. 4. Mix the ground beef mixture, rice, Cheddar cheese, tomato sauce, relish, ketchup, Worcestershire sauce, and mustard in a large bowl. 5. Spoon the meat and rice mixture equally into the peppers. 6. Place the stuffed peppers in the air fryer basket. Air fry them at 180°C for 10 to 15 minutes, until golden brown on top. 7. Top each stuffed pepper with the shredded lettuce and diced tomatoes and serve.
Per Serving: Calories 334; Fat 8.84g; Sodium 945mg; Carbs 32.11g; Fibre 4.6g; Sugar 12.38g; Protein 32.15g

Mini Beef Meatloaves

Prep Time: 10 minutes | **Cook Time:** 20 minutes | **Serves:** 4

Olive oil
455g of lean ground beef
1 egg, beaten
120g of wholewheat breadcrumbs
60ml of low-fat evaporated milk
60ml plus 2 tablespoons of barbeque sauce, divided
1 teaspoon of onion powder
1 teaspoon of salt
½ teaspoon of freshly ground black pepper

1. Lightly spray the air fryer basket with olive oil. 2. Combine the ground beef, egg, breadcrumbs, milk, 60ml of barbeque sauce, onion powder, salt, and pepper in a large bowl. 3. Divide the beef mixture into four small meatloaf shapes, spreading each meatloaf with ½ tablespoon of the remaining barbeque sauce. 4. Place the meatloaves in the air fryer basket in a single layer. 5. Air fry the meatloaves

at 175°C for 15 to 20 minutes, until the internal temperature reaches at least 70°C. 6. Serve and enjoy.
Per Serving: Calories 298; Fat 9.83g; Sodium 1041mg; Carbs 22.21g; Fibre 1.7g; Sugar 2.81g; Protein 30.06g

Mushroom-Beef Balls

Prep Time: 15 minutes | **Cook Time:** 15 minutes | **Serves:** 6

Olive oil
910g of lean ground beef
70g of finely chopped mushrooms
4 tablespoons of chopped parsley
2 eggs, beaten
2 teaspoons of salt
1 teaspoon of freshly ground black pepper
120g of wholewheat breadcrumbs

1. Lightly spray the air fryer basket with olive oil. 2. Gently mix the beef, mushrooms, parsley, eggs, salt, and pepper in a large bowl, then add the breadcrumbs and mix them until the breadcrumbs are no longer dry. Do not overmix. 3. Divide the mixture into 24 meatballs. 4. Working in batches, arrange the meatballs in the fryer basket in a single layer, and lightly spray them with olive oil. 5. Air fry the meatballs at 200°C for 10 to 15 minutes until the internal temperature reaches at least 70°C, shaking the basket every 5 minutes for even cooking. 6. Serve and enjoy.
Per Serving: Calories 301; Fat 10.73g; Sodium 1030mg; Carbs 13.88g; Fibre 1.1g; Sugar 1.41g; Protein 37.07g

Steak-Veggie Kebabs

Prep Time: 10 minutes | **Cook Time:** 15 minutes | **Serves:** 4

120ml of soy sauce
3 tablespoons of lemon juice
2 tablespoons of Worcestershire sauce
2 tablespoons of Dijon mustard
1 teaspoon of minced garlic
¾ teaspoon of freshly ground black pepper
455g sirloin steak, cut into 25mm cubes
1 medium red bell pepper, cut into big chunks

1 medium green bell pepper, cut into big chunks
1 medium red onion, cut into big chunks
Olive oil

1. Mix the soy sauce, lemon juice, Worcestershire sauce, Dijon mustard, garlic, and black pepper in a small bowl. 2. Apportion the marinade between two large zip-top plastic bags. 3. Place the steak in one of the bags, seal, and refrigerate for at least 2 hours. Place the vegetables in the other bag, seal, and refrigerate for 1 hour. 3. Soak the skewers in water for at least 30 minutes if using wooden skewers. 4. Lightly spray the air fryer basket with olive oil. 5. Thread the steak and veggies alternately onto the skewers. 6. Working in batches, arrange the skewers in the oiled fryer basket in a single layer. 7. Air fry them at 175°C for 15 minutes, until the steak has been cooked to your taste, flipping them over and lightly spraying some olive oil halfway through. 8. The internal temperature should read 50°C for rare, 55°C for medium-rare, 60°C for medium and 65°C for medium-well. 9. When done, serve and enjoy.
Per Serving: Calories 268; Fat 10.28g; Sodium 745mg; Carbs 16.83g; Fibre 2.4g; Sugar 10.36g; Protein 26.43g

Mushroom Steak Bites

Prep Time: 65 minutes | **Cook Time:** 20 minutes | **Serves:** 4

455g sirloin steak, cut into 15mm cubes
230g of mushrooms, sliced
1 tablespoon of Worcestershire sauce
1 tablespoon of balsamic vinegar
1 tablespoon of soy sauce
1 tablespoon of olive oil, plus more for spraying
1 teaspoon of Dijon mustard
1 teaspoon of minced garlic
Salt
Freshly ground black pepper

1. Toss the steak and mushrooms with Worcestershire sauce, balsamic vinegar, soy sauce, olive oil, Dijon mustard, garlic, salt, and pepper in a large zip-top plastic bag, seal

the bag and refrigerate for at least 1 hour or overnight. 2. Lightly spray the air fryer basket with olive oil. 3. Working in batches, add the steak and mushrooms to the fryer basket in an even layer. 4. Air fry them at 200°C for 20 minutes until the steak has been cooked to your taste, shaking the basket halfway through (the internal temperature should read 50°C for rare, 55°C for medium-rare, 60°C for medium and 65°C for medium-well). 5. Serve warm.

Per Serving: Calories 187; Fat 7.27g; Sodium 249mg; Carbs 4.67g; Fibre 0.7g; Sugar 2.93g; Protein 25.06g

Beef and Broccoli Bowls

Prep Time: 2 hours 15 minutes | **Cook Time:** 15 minutes | **Serves:** 4

3 tablespoons of dry sherry
60ml of soy sauce
4 garlic cloves, minced
1 tablespoon of sesame oil
½ teaspoon of red pepper flakes
455g flank or skirt steak, trimmed and cut into strips
Olive oil
230g of broccoli florets
60ml of beef broth
2 teaspoons of cornflour

1. To make the marinade, mix the sherry, soy sauce, garlic, sesame oil, and red pepper flakes in a small bowl. 2. Place the steak strips and 3 tablespoons of the marinade in a large zip-top plastic bag, seal, shake the bag, and then refrigerate for at least 2 hours. 3. Lightly spray the air fryer basket with olive oil. 4. Add half the steak to the fryer basket along with half the broccoli florets. Lightly spray them with olive oil. 5. Air fry them at 185°C for 15 minutes, shaking the basket to redistribute. 6. Do the same with the remaining steak and broccoli. 7. Transfer the steak and broccoli to a large bowl. 8. While the steak is cooking, add the broth and the remaining marinade to a small saucepan over medium-high heat, and bring to a boil. 9. Combine the cornflour and 1 tablespoon of water to create a slurry in a small ball, then

add the slurry to the saucepan and simmer for a few seconds to 1 minute until the sauce starts to thicken, stirring occasionally. 10. Pour the sauce over the cooked steak and broccoli and toss to evenly coat.

Per Serving: Calories 281; Fat 13.41g; Sodium 344mg; Carbs 12.26g; Fibre 2.4g; Sugar 5.91g; Protein 27.67g

BBQ Beef Bowls

Prep Time: 2 hours 10 minutes | **Cook Time:** 25 minutes | **Serves:** 4

120ml of soy sauce
2 tablespoons of brown sugar
2 tablespoons of red wine vinegar or rice vinegar
1 tablespoon of olive oil, plus more for spraying
1 tablespoon of sesame oil
455g skirt steak, sliced very thin against the grain
2 teaspoons cornflour
500g of cooked brown rice
140g of steamed broccoli florets

1. Toss the steak slices with the soy sauce, brown sugar, vinegar, olive oil, and sesame oil in a large bowl, then cover the bowl with plastic wrap, and refrigerate for at least 30 minutes or up to 2 hours. 2. Lightly spray the air fryer basket with olive oil. 3. Remove as much marinade as possible from the steak. Reserve any leftover marinade. 4. Place the steak in the air fryer basket in a single layer. 5. Air fry them at 195°C for 20 minutes, flipping the steak over halfway through. 6. The internal temperature should read 50°C for rare, 55°C for medium-rare, 60°C for medium, and 65°C for medium-well. 7. Transfer the steak to a large bowl and set aside. 8. Combine the cornflour and 1 tablespoon of water to create a slurry in a small bowl. 9. Bring the remaining marinade to a boil in a small saucepan over medium-high heat, add the slurry to the marinade, lower the heat to medium-low, and simmer them for a few seconds to 1 minutes until the sauce starts to thicken, stirring occasionally. 10. Pour the sauce over the steak and stir to combine. 11.

To assemble the bowls, spoon 125g of the cooked brown rice and 35g of broccoli into each of four bowls, and top with the steak.
Per Serving: Calories 443; Fat 19.12g; Sodium 550mg; Carbs 36.64g; Fibre 3g; Sugar 10.47g; Protein 29.48g

Beef Chimichangas

Prep Time: 10 minutes | **Cook Time:** 20 minutes | **Serves:** 4

Olive oil
455g of lean ground beef
1 tablespoon of taco seasoning
115g of salsa
1 (455g) can of fat-free refried beans
4 large wholewheat tortillas
55g of shredded Cheddar cheese

1. Lightly spray the air fryer basket with olive oil. 2. Cook the ground beef in a large skillet over medium heat for 5 minutes, until browned, add the taco seasoning and salsa, and stir to combine. Set aside after cooking. 3. Spread ¼ of the refried beans onto each tortilla, leaving a 15mm border around the edge. Add ¼ of the ground beef mixture to each tortilla and sprinkle with 2 tablespoons of Cheddar cheese. 4. Fold the opposite sides of the tortilla in and roll up. 5. Place the chimichangas in the fryer basket, with seam side down, and lightly spray them with olive oil. 6. Air fry them at 180°C for 5 to 10 minutes until golden brown.
Per Serving: Calories 416; Fat 12.62g; Sodium 1322mg; Carbs 39.07g; Fibre 10.2g; Sugar 4.21g; Protein 36.83g

Tasty Steak Fingers

Prep Time: 15 minutes | **Cook Time:** 15 minutes | **Serves:** 4

Olive oil
70g of wholewheat flour
1 teaspoon of seasoned salt
½ teaspoon of freshly ground black pepper
¼ teaspoon of cayenne pepper
2 eggs, beaten
120ml of low-fat milk
455g cube steak, cut into 25mm-wide strips

1. Lightly spray the air fryer basket with olive oil. 2. Mix the flour, salt, black pepper, and cayenne in a shallow bowl. 3. Beat the eggs and milk in another bowl. 4. Dredge the steak strips in the flour mixture, then coat them with the egg mixture, and finally dredge them in the flour mixture once more to coat completely. 5. Place the steak strips in the air fryer basket in a single layer, and spray lightly with olive oil. 6. Air fry them at 180°C for 15 minutes until golden brown and crispy, flipping them over and lightly spraying with olive oil halfway through. 7. Serve warm.
Per Serving: Calories 269; Fat 10.03g; Sodium 836mg; Carbs 11.37g; Fibre 1.7g; Sugar 0.25g; Protein 32.44g

Sirloin Steak Roll-Ups

Prep Time: 60 minutes | **Cook Time:** 20 minutes | **Serves:** 4

680g sirloin steak, cut into slices
2 tablespoons Worcestershire sauce
½ tablespoon garlic powder
½ tablespoon onion powder
2 medium peppers of any colour, cut into thin strips
55g shredded mozzarella cheese
Salt
Freshly ground black pepper
Olive oil

1. Pound the steaks very thin. 2. To make the marinade, mix the Worcestershire sauce, garlic powder, and onion powder in a small bowl. 3. Place the steaks and marinade in a large zip-top plastic bag, seal, and refrigerate the for at least 30 minutes. 4. Soak 8 toothpicks in water for 15 to 20 minutes. 5. Lightly spray the air fryer basket with olive oil. 6. Place ¼ of the peppers and ¼ of the mozzarella cheese in the centre of each steak, and season them with salt and black pepper. 7. Roll each steak up tightly and secure with 2 toothpicks, then place them in the air fryer basket in a single layer with toothpick-side down. 8. Air fry them at 200°C for 20 minutes until the meat reaches an internal temperature of at least 65°C, flipping them

over halfway through cooking. 9. Let the roll-ups rest for 10 minutes before serving.
Per Serving: Calories 282; Fat 9.05g; Sodium 327mg; Carbs 5.88g; Fibre 0.8g; Sugar 2.3g; Protein 42.49g

Simple Rib Eye Steak

Prep Time: 5 minutes | **Cook Time:** 15 minutes | **Serves:** 4

Olive oil
2 (200g) rib eye steaks
1 tablespoon olive oil
1 teaspoon garlic salt
Salt
Freshly ground black pepper

1. Lightly spray the air fryer basket with olive oil. 2. Drizzle the steaks with olive oil on both sides, and season them with garlic salt, salt, and pepper on bother sides. 3. Place the steaks in the air fryer basket in a single layer. 4. Air fry them at 200°C for 15 minutes until they reach your desired level of doneness, flipping them over halfway through cooking. 5. The steak should be at least 50°C for rare, 55°C for medium rare, 60°C for medium, and 65°C for medium well. 6. Serve and enjoy.
Per Serving: Calories 188; Fat 16.39g; Sodium 71mg; Carbs 0.25g; Fibre 0g; Sugar 0.01g; Protein 10.21g

Glazed Pork-Apple Skewers

Prep Time: 10 minutes | **Cook Time:** 20 minutes | **Serves:** 4

For the glaze
160g sugar-free apricot jam
3 tablespoons lemon juice
2 tablespoons Dijon mustard
2 teaspoons dried rosemary
1 teaspoon lemon zest
For the kebabs
Olive oil
2 gala apples, cored and sliced into wedges
454g pork tenderloin, cut into 2.5cm pieces
Salt
Freshly ground black pepper

1. To make the glaze, mix the apricot jam, lemon juice, Dijon mustard, rosemary, and lemon zest in a small bowl. Set aside. 2. Lightly spray the air fryer basket with olive oil. 3.Cut each wedge of apple in half crosswise into chunks. 4. If using wooden skewers, soak them in water for at least 30 minutes before using. 5. Thread the pork and apples alternately onto the skewers. Spray lightly all over with olive oil and season with salt and pepper. 6. Place the skewers in the fryer basket in a single layer, and air fry them at 175°C for 10 minutes, generously brushing the glaze on the skewers during cooking. 8. When the cooking time is up, increase the temperature to 185°C, and resume cooking the skewers for 10 minutes until the pork reaches an internal temperature of at least 60°C, flipping them over and brushing them again with the glaze halfway through. 9. Serve hot.
Per Serving: Calories 229; Fat 5.57g; Sodium 203mg; Carbs 14.11g; Fibre 2.6g; Sugar 9.85g; Protein 30.34g

Panko Breaded Pork Cutlets

Prep Time: 15 minutes | **Cook Time:** 15 minutes | **Serves:** 4

Olive oil
55g whole wheat-panko bread crumbs
½ teaspoon garlic powder
2 eggs, beaten
4 (2.5cm) boneless pork chops, fat trimmed
Salt
Freshly ground black pepper

1. Lightly spray the air fryer basket with olive oil. 2. Mix the panko bread crumbs and garlic powder in a shallow bowl. 3. Beat the eggs with 1 teaspoon of water in another bowl. 4. Place the pork chops between two sheets of parchment paper or plastic wrap. 5. Pound the pork chops until they are 0.6cm thick, and season them with salt and pepper. 6. Coat the pork in the egg mixture and shake off any excess, then dredge them in the bread crumb mixture. 7. Place the pork in the fryer basket in a single layer, and lightly spray the pork cutlets with olive oil. 8. Air fry them at 200°C for 15 minutes until they have

an internal temperature of at least 60°C, flipping them and lightly spraying them with olive oil halfway through cooking. 9. Serve hot.
Per Serving: Calories 340; Fat 9.83g; Sodium 161mg; Carbs 12.89g; Fibre 0.5g; Sugar 0.14g; Protein 46.34g

Chili Pork Loin

Prep Time: 70 minutes | **Cook Time:** 30 minutes | **Serves:** 4

1 tablespoon lime juice
1 tablespoon olive oil, plus more for spraying
½ tablespoon soy sauce
½ tablespoon chili powder
¼ tablespoon minced garlic
454g boneless pork tenderloin

1. Lightly spray the air fryer basket with olive oil. 2. Mix pork with the lime juice, olive oil, soy sauce, chili powder, and garlic in a large zip-top plastic bag, then seal the bag, and refrigerate them for at least 1 hour or overnight. 3. Shake off any excess marinade from the pork, and place it in the air fryer basket. 4. Air fry the pork at 200°C for 15 minutes. 5. Flip the tenderloin over and cook until the pork for an additional 5 minutes until it reaches an internal temperature of at least 60°C. If necessary, continue to cook in 2- to 3-minute intervals until it reaches the proper temperature. 5. Let the tenderloin rest for 10 minutes before cutting into slices and serving.
Per Serving: Calories 177; Fat 12.75g; Sodium 1336mg; Carbs 3.09g; Fibre 0.4g; Sugar 2.14g; Protein 19.67g

Spiced Pork Chops

Prep Time: 10 minutes | **Cook Time:** 15 minutes | **Serves:** 4

1 tablespoon olive oil, plus more for spraying
3 tablespoons brown sugar
½ teaspoon cayenne pepper
½ teaspoon garlic powder
½ teaspoon salt
¼ teaspoon freshly ground black pepper
4 thin boneless pork chops, trimmed of excess fat

1. Lightly spray the air fryer basket with olive oil. 2. Mix the brown sugar, 1 tablespoon of olive oil, cayenne pepper, garlic powder, salt, and black pepper in a small bowl. 3. Coat each pork chop with the marinade, shaking them to remove any excess, and place them in the air fryer basket in a single layer. 4. Air fry them at 185°C for 15 minutes until the chops reach an internal temperature of 60°C, flipping them and brushing them with more marinade halfway through cooking. 5. Serve warm.
Per Serving: Calories 291; Fat 9.75g; Sodium 382mg; Carbs 6.52g; Fibre 0.1g; Sugar 5.9g; Protein 41.57g

Breaded Thin Pork Chops

Prep Time: 10 minutes | **Cook Time:** 15 minutes | **Serves:** 4

Olive oil
2 eggs, beaten
30g whole-wheat bread crumbs
1 sachet zesty Italian dressing mix
4 thin boneless pork chops, trimmed of excess fat
Salt
Freshly ground black pepper

1. Lightly spray the air fryer basket with olive oil. 2. Place the eggs in a shallow bowl. 3. Mix the bread crumbs and Italian dressing mix in a separate shallow bowl. 4. Season the pork chops with salt and pepper, then coat the pork chops in the egg, shaking off any excess, and dredge them in the bread crumb mixture. 5. Place the pork chops in the fryer basket in a single layer, and spray lightly with olive oil. 6. Air fry them at 185°C for 15 minutes until they reach an internal temperature of at least 60°C, flipping them over and lightly spraying them with olive oil halfway through cooking.
Per Serving: Calories 306; Fat 10.16g; Sodium 222mg; Carbs 5.18g; Fibre 0.3g; Sugar 0.63g; Protein 45.13g

Pork Meatball Bowl

Prep Time: 15 minutes | **Cook Time:** 15 minutes | **Serves:** 4

Olive oil
900g lean pork mince
2 eggs, beaten
100g whole-wheat panko bread crumbs
1 spring onion, thinly sliced
2 teaspoons soy sauce
2 teaspoons minced garlic
½ teaspoon ground ginger
320g cooked rice noodles (cooked according to package directions)
130g peeled and shredded carrots
120g peeled and thinly sliced cucumber
240ml light Asian sesame dressing

1. Lightly spray the air fryer basket with olive oil. 2. Mix the pork, eggs, bread crumbs, spring onion, soy sauce, garlic, and ginger in a large bowl, then make the mixture into 24 meatballs. 3. Place the meatballs in a single layer in the fryer basket, and lightly spray meatballs with olive oil. 5. Air fry the meatballs at 200°C for 10 to 15 minutes until they reach an internal temperature of at least 60°C, shaking the basket every 5 minutes for even cooking. 6. To assemble the bowls, divide rice noodles, carrots, and cucumber between 4 bowls. Drizzle each bowl with sesame dressing and top with 6 meatballs. Enjoy.
Per Serving: Calories 642; Fat 15.36g; Sodium 1060mg; Carbs 68.39g; Fibre 3.8g; Sugar 14.41g; Protein 57.03g

Pineapple Pork Sliders

Prep Time: 15 minutes | **Cook Time:** 15 minutes | **Serves:** 4
Olive oil
90g crushed pineapple, drained
454g lean pork mince
1 teaspoon Worcestershire sauce
½ teaspoon garlic powder
½ teaspoon salt
½ teaspoon freshly ground black pepper
Pinch of cayenne pepper
8 whole-wheat slider buns

1. Lightly spray the air fryer basket with olive oil. 2. Mix the pineapple, pork, Worcestershire sauce, garlic powder, salt, and pepper

in a large bowl, then form the mixture into 8 patties. 3. Place the patties in the fryer basket in a single layer and spray lightly with olive oil. 4. Air fry the patties at 185°C for 15 minutes until they reach an internal temperature of at least 60°C, flipping them over and lightly spraying them with olive oil halfway through. 5. Place the cooked patties on the slider buns and serve.
Per Serving: Calories 269; Fat 7.11g; Sodium 577mg; Carbs 23.78g; Fibre 1.6g; Sugar 4.5g; Protein 27.74g

Pork and Salad

Prep Time: 10 minutes | **Cook Time:** 15 minutes | **Serves:** 4
900g pork tenderloin, cut into 1-inch slices
1 teaspoon olive oil
1 teaspoon dried marjoram
⅛ teaspoon freshly ground black pepper
85g mixed salad leaves
1 red pepper, sliced
1 (227g) packet button mushrooms, sliced
80ml low-sodium low-fat vinaigrette dressing

1. Coat the pork slices with olive oil and rub them with the marjoram and pepper. 2. Grill the pork slices in the air fryer at 400°F/ 200°C for 4 to 6 minutes until they reach an internal temperature of at least 145°F/ 60°C. 3. Mix the salad leaves, red pepper, and mushrooms in a serving bowl. 4. When the pork is cooked, add the slices to the salad, drizzle with the vinaigrette and toss gently. Enjoy.
Per Serving: Calories 322; Fat 8.83g; Sodium 223mg; Carbs 5.82g; Fiber 3g; Sugar 1.79g; Protein 53.32g

Coconut Pork Satay

Prep Time: 15 minutes | **Cook Time:** 15 minutes | **Serves:** 4
1 (454g) pork tenderloin, cut into 1½-inch cubes
26g chopped onion
2 garlic cloves, chopped
1 jalapeño pepper, chopped
2 tablespoons freshly squeezed lime juice

2 tablespoons coconut milk
2 tablespoons unsalted peanut butter
2 teaspoons curry powder

1. Combine the pork, onion, garlic, jalapeño, lime juice, coconut milk, peanut butter, and curry powder in a medium bowl. Let it marinade for 10 minutes at room temperature. 2. Remove the pork from the marinade and reserve the marinade. 3. Thread the pork onto about 8 bamboo (pre-soaked in water for 30 minutes to avoid burning) or metal skewers. 4. Grill them at 380°F/ 195°C for 9 to 14 minutes until they reach an internal temperature of at least 145°F/ 60°C. Brush once with the reserved marinade during cooking. 5. Discard any remaining marinade after cooking.
Per Serving: Calories 226; Fat 8.51g; Sodium 71mg; Carbs 4.74g; Fiber 1.2g; Sugar 1.84g; Protein 32.07g

Pork Cabbage Burgers

Prep Time: 20 minutes | **Cook Time:** 9 minutes | **Serves:** 4
125ml Greek yogurt
2 tablespoons low-sodium mustard, divided
1 tablespoon lemon juice
43g sliced red cabbage
43g grated carrots
454g lean minced pork
½ teaspoon paprika
14g mixed baby lettuce leaves
2 small tomatoes, sliced
8 small low-sodium whole-wheat sandwich buns, cut in half

1. Mix the yogurt, 1 tablespoon of the mustard, lemon juice, cabbage, and carrots in a small bowl, and then place the bowl in fridge. 2. Toss the pork with the remaining mustard, and the paprika in a medium bowl, then form the mixture into 8 small patties. 3. Put the sliders in the air fryer basket. Grill them at 400°F/ 200°C for 7 to 9 minutes until the sliders register 165°F/ 75°C. 4. Assemble the burgers by placing some of the lettuce leaves on a bun bottom. Top with a tomato slice, a

burger, and the cabbage mixture. Add the bun top and serve immediately.
Per Serving: Calories 171; Fat 4.85g; Sodium 105mg; Carbs 6.8g; Fiber 1.5g; Sugar 3.99g; Protein 26.09g

Mustard Pork Tenderloin

Prep Time: 10 minutes | **Cook Time:** 16 minutes | **Serves:** 4
3 tablespoons low-sodium grainy mustard
2 teaspoons olive oil
¼ teaspoon dry mustard powder
1 (454g) pork tenderloin, silver skin and excess fat trimmed and discarded
2 slices low-sodium whole-wheat bread, crumbled
15g ground walnuts
2 tablespoons corn flour

1. Mix the mustard, olive oil, and mustard powder in a small bowl. Spread this mixture over the pork. 2. Mix the breadcrumbs, walnuts, and corn flour on a plate. 3. Dip the mustard-coated pork into the crumb mixture to coat. 4. Air-fry the pork at 400°F/ 200°C for 12 to 16 minutes until it registers at least 145°F/ 60°C. 5. Slice to serve after cooking.
Per Serving: Calories 215; Fat 12.75g; Sodium 362mg; Carbs 0.11g; Fiber 0g; Sugar 0g; Protein 23.66g

Pork Tenderloin with Apple Slices

Prep Time: 10 minutes | **Cook Time:** 20 minutes | **Serves:** 4
1 (454g) pork tenderloin, cut into 4 pieces
1 tablespoon apple butter (or apple sauce)
2 teaspoons olive oil
2 Granny Smith apples, sliced
3 celery sticks, sliced
1 onion, sliced
½ teaspoon dried marjoram
80ml apple juice

1. Rub each piece of pork with the apple butter and olive oil. 2. Mix the pork, apples, celery, onion, marjoram, and apple juice in a suitable bowl. 3. Place the bowl into the air

fryer and roast the mixture at 400°F/ 200°C for 14 to 19 minutes until the pork reaches at least 145°F/ 60°C and the apples and vegetables are tender. 4. Stir them halfway through cooking. 5. Serve immediately.
Per Serving: Calories 260; Fat 8.37g; Sodium 78mg; Carbs 14.31g; Fiber 2.7g; Sugar 10.24g; Protein 30.3g

Grilled Pork Tenderloin

Prep Time: 15 minutes | **Cook Time:** 9 to 11 minutes | **Serves:** 4

1 tablespoon brown sugar
2 teaspoons espresso powder
1 teaspoon ground paprika
½ teaspoon dried marjoram
1 tablespoon honey
1 tablespoon freshly squeezed lemon juice
2 teaspoons olive oil
1 (454g) pork tenderloin

1. Mix the brown sugar, espresso powder, paprika, marjoram, honey, lemon juice, and olive oil in a small bowl. 2. Spread the honey mixture over the pork and let it stand for 10 minutes at room temperature. 3. Roast the tenderloin in the air fryer at 400°F/ 200°C for 9 to 11 minutes until the pork registers an internal temperature of at least 145°F/ 60°C. 4. Slice the meat after cooking and serve hot.
Per Serving: Calories 174; Fat 4.81g; Sodium 62mg; Carbs 7.89g; Fiber 0.4g; Sugar 6.51g; Protein 24g

Pork Tenderloin with Potatoes

Prep Time: 5 minutes | **Cook Time:** 25 minutes | **Serves:** 4

280g King Edward potatoes, rinsed and dried
2 teaspoons olive oil
1 (454g) pork tenderloin, cut into 1-inch cubes
1 onion, chopped
1 red pepper, chopped
2 garlic cloves, chopped
½ teaspoon dried oregano
2 tablespoons low-sodium chicken broth

1. Toss the potatoes and olive oil in a medium bowl, then transfer them to the air fryer basket. 2. Roast the potatoes at 370°F/ 185°C for 15 minutes. 3. Mix the potatoes, pork, onion, red pepper, garlic, and oregano in a suitable bowl, and drizzle with the chicken broth. 4. Put the bowl in the air fryer basket, then roast the mixture for about 10 minutes more, until the potatoes are tender, and pork reaches an internal temperature of at least 145°F/ 60°C. Shaking the basket once during cooking. 5. Serve immediately.
Per Serving: Calories 221; Fat 4.91g; Sodium 69mg; Carbs 17.33g; Fiber 2.4g; Sugar 2.38g; Protein 26.04g

Pork-Fruit Kebabs

Prep Time: 15 minutes | **Cook Time:** 9 to 12 minutes | **Serves:** 4

105g apricot jam
2 tablespoons freshly squeezed lemon juice
2 teaspoons olive oil
½ teaspoon dried tarragon
1 (454g) pork tenderloin, cut into 1-inch cubes
4 plums, pitted and quartered
4 small apricots, pitted and halved

1. Mix the jam, lemon juice, olive oil, and tarragon in a large bowl, then coat the pork cubes with the mixture. Let it stand for 10 minutes at room temperature. 2. Alternating the items, thread the pork, plums, and apricots onto 4 metal skewers. 3. Brush them with any remaining jam mixture. Discard any remaining marinade. 4. Grill the kebabs in the air fryer at 380°F/ 195°C for 9 to 12 minutes, until the pork cubes reach an internal temperature of 145°F/ 60°C, and the fruit is tender. 5. Serve hot.
Per Serving: Calories 267; Fat 4.97g; Sodium 80mg; Carbs 32.15g; Fiber 1.2g; Sugar 25.15g; Protein 24.64g

Steak-Vegetable Kebabs

Prep Time: 15 minutes | **Cook Time:** 5 to 7 minutes | **Serves:** 4

2 tablespoons balsamic vinegar

2 teaspoons olive oil
½ teaspoon dried marjoram
⅛ teaspoon freshly ground black pepper
¾ pound round steak, cut into 1-inch pieces
1 red pepper, sliced
16 button mushrooms
200g cherry tomatoes

1. Stir the balsamic vinegar, olive oil, marjoram, and black pepper in a medium bowl, then coat the steak pieces with the mixture. Let it stand for 10 minutes at room temperature. 2. Alternating items, thread the beef, red pepper, mushrooms, and tomatoes onto 8 bamboo or metal skewers that fit in the air fryer. 3. Grill them in the air fryer at 390°F/ 200°C for 5 to 7 minutes, until the beef pieces are browned and reach an internal temperature of at least 145°F/ 60°C. 4. Serve immediately.
Per Serving: Calories 182; Fat 8.23g; Sodium 62mg; Carbs 6.26g; Fiber 1.4g; Sugar 4.2g; Protein 20.89g

Simple Grilled Steaks

Prep Time: 10 minutes | **Cook Time:** 20 minutes | **Serves:** 4
2 tablespoons low-sodium salsa
1 tablespoon chopped chipotle pepper
1 tablespoon apple cider vinegar
1 teaspoon ground cumin
⅛ teaspoon freshly ground black pepper
⅛ teaspoon red pepper flakes
340g sirloin tip steak, cut into 4 pieces and gently pounded to about ⅓ inch thick

1. Thoroughly mix the salsa, chipotle pepper, cider vinegar, cumin, black pepper, and red pepper flakes in a small bowl. Rub this mixture into both sides of each steak piece. Let it stand for 15 minutes at room temperature. 2. Working in batches, grill the steaks in the air fryer at 390°F/ 200°C for 6 to 9 minutes until they reach at least 145°F/ 60°C on a meat thermometer. 3. Remove the steaks to a clean plate and cover with tin foil to keep warm. Repeat with the remaining steaks. 4. Slice the steaks thinly against the grain and serve.

Per Serving: Calories 134; Fat 5.1g; Sodium 55mg; Carbs 3.86g; Fiber 0.3g; Sugar 2.48g; Protein 18.6g

Greek Vegetable Beef Bowl

Prep Time: 10 minutes | **Cook Time:** 9 to 19 minutes | **Serves:** 4
225g lean beef mince
2 medium tomatoes, chopped
1 onion, chopped
2 garlic cloves, minced
60g fresh baby spinach
2 tablespoons freshly squeezed lemon juice
80ml beef stock
2 tablespoons crumbled low-sodium feta cheese

1. Crumble the beef in a 15-by-5-cm metal pan. Cook the beef in the air fryer at 185°C for 3 to 7 minutes until browned, stirring once during cooking. Drain off any fat or liquid. 2. Add the tomatoes, onion, and garlic to the pan, and air-fry them for 4 to 8 minutes more until the onion is tender. 3. Add the spinach, lemon juice, and beef stock, then air-fry them for 2 to 4 minutes more until the spinach is wilted. 4. Sprinkle with the feta cheese, and serve immediately.
Per Serving: Calories 201; Fat 10.78g; Sodium 249mg; Carbs 8.6g; Fibre 1.6g; Sugar 3.25g; Protein 17.82g

Light Herbed Beef Meatballs

Prep Time: 10 minutes | **Cook Time:** 12 to 17 minutes | **Serves:** 4
1 medium onion, minced
2 garlic cloves, minced
1 teaspoon olive oil
1 slice low-sodium whole-wheat bread, crumbled
3 tablespoons low fat milk
1 teaspoon dried marjoram
1 teaspoon dried basil
454g lean beef mince

1. Combine the onion, garlic, and olive oil in a 15-by-5-cm pan, then air-fry them at 195°C for 2 to 4 minutes until the vegetables are

crisp-tender. 2. Transfer the vegetables to a medium bowl, and add the bread crumbs, milk, marjoram, and basil, mix them well; add the beef mince, then gently but thoroughly combine them. 3. Form the meat mixture into about 24 (2.5cm) meatballs. 4. Working in batches, bake the meatballs in the air fryer for 12 to 17 minutes until they reach 70°C on a meat thermometer. 5. Serve immediately.

Per Serving: Calories 200; Fat 7.5g; Sodium 118mg; Carbs 7.19g; Fibre 1.1g; Sugar 2.11g; Protein 26.09g

Beef-Stuffed Peppers

Prep Time: 10 minutes | **Cook Time:** 11 to 16 minutes | **Serves:** 4

4 medium peppers, any colours, rinsed, tops removed
1 medium onion, chopped
55g grated carrot
2 teaspoons olive oil
2 medium beef tomatoes, chopped
195g cooked brown rice
140g chopped cooked roast beef
1 teaspoon dried marjoram

1. Remove the stems from the pepper tops and chop the tops. 2. Combine the chopped pepper tops, onion, carrot, and olive oil in a 15-by-5-cm pan, then cook them in the air fryer at 200°C for 2 to 4 minutes until the vegetables are crisp-tender. 3. Transfer the vegetables to a medium bowl, mix in the tomatoes, brown rice, roast beef, and marjoram. 4. Stuff the vegetable mixture into the peppers, and place the peppers in the air fryer basket. 5. Bake them at 200°C for 11 to 16 minutes until they are tender and the filling is hot. 6. Serve immediately.

Per Serving: Calories 164; Fat 4.38g; Sodium 33mg; Carbs 28.1g; Fibre 3.3g; Sugar 6.43g; Protein 5.72g

Beef Broccoli in Stock

Prep Time: 10 minutes | **Cook Time:** 14 to 18 minutes | **Serves:** 4

2 tablespoons cornflour

120ml beef stock
1 teaspoon low-sodium soy sauce
300g sirloin strip steak, cut into 2.5cm cubes
220g broccoli florets
1 onion, chopped
70g sliced cremini mushrooms
1 tablespoon grated fresh ginger
Brown rice, cooked (optional)

1. Stir the cornflour, beef stock, and soy sauce in a medium bowl, then toss the beef with the mixture. Let stand for 5 minutes at room temperature. 2. Transfer the beef from the stock mixture into a medium metal bowl. Reserve the stock. 3. Add the broccoli, onion, mushrooms, and ginger to the beef. 4. Place the bowl into the air fryer, and cook them at 200°C for 12 to 15 minutes until the beef reaches at least 60°C on a meat thermometer and the vegetables are tender. 5. Add the reserved stock and cook for 2 to 3 minutes more until the sauce boils. 6. Serve immediately over hot cooked brown rice (optional).

Per Serving: Calories 155; Fat 3.18g; Sodium 105mg; Carbs 10.32g; Fibre 1.3g; Sugar 1.59g; Protein 22.25g

Stir-Fried Beef and Fruit

Prep Time: 15 minutes | **Cook Time:** 6 to 11 minutes | **Serves:** 4

300g sirloin tip steak, thinly sliced
1 tablespoon freshly squeezed lime juice
190g canned mandarin orange segments, drained, juice reserved
180g canned pineapple chunks, drained, juice reserved
1 teaspoon low-sodium soy sauce
1 tablespoon cornflour
1 teaspoon olive oil
2 spring onions, white and green parts, sliced
Brown rice, cooked (optional)

1. Mix the steak with the lime juice in a medium bowl. Set aside. 2. Thoroughly mix 3 tablespoons of reserved mandarin orange juice, 3 tablespoons of reserved pineapple juice, the soy sauce, and cornflour in a small bowl. 3. Drain the beef and transfer it to a medium

metal bowl, reserving the juice. Stir the reserved juice into the mandarin-pineapple juice mixture. 4. Add the olive oil and spring onions to the steak. Place the metal bowl in the air fryer, and cook them at 185°C for 3 to 4 minutes until the steak is almost cooked, shaking the basket once during cooking. 5. Stir in the mandarin oranges, pineapple, and juice mixture, and cook them for 3 to 7 minutes more until the sauce is bubbling and the beef is tender and reaches at least 60°C on a meat thermometer. 6. Stir and serve over hot cooked brown rice (optional).
Per Serving: Calories 363; Fat 24.32g; Sodium 102mg; Carbs 22.86g; Fibre 1.8g; Sugar 18.33g; Protein 14.93g

Parmesan Beef Risotto

Prep Time: 6 minutes | **Cook Time:** 20 to 24 minutes | **Serves:** 4

2 teaspoons olive oil
1 onion, finely chopped
3 garlic cloves, minced
50g chopped red pepper
150g short-grain rice
300ml low-sodium beef stock
75g chopped cooked roast beef
3 tablespoons grated Parmesan cheese

1. Combine the olive oil, onion, garlic, and red pepper in a 15-by-5-cm pan. 2. Place the pan in the air fryer, and cook them at 200°C for 2 minutes until the vegetables are crisp-tender. 3. Remove the pan from the air fryer, add the rice, beef stock, and roast beef, then return the pan to the air fryer. 4. Bake them for 18 to 22 minutes until the rice is tender and the beef reaches at least 60°C on a meat thermometer, stirring once during cooking. 4. Stir in the Parmesan cheese after cooking and serve immediately.
Per Serving: Calories 395; Fat 11.82g; Sodium 156mg; Carbs 45.24g; Fibre 2.1g; Sugar 5.13g; Protein 28.08g

Butter Ribeye Steak

Prep Time: 5 minutes | **Cook Time:** 10 minutes | **Serves:** 2

1 tablespoon water
1 (300g) ribeye steak, 2.5cm thick
2 teaspoons Montreal steak seasoning
1 tablespoon unsalted butter, cut in half
1 teaspoon chopped fresh dill

1. Preheat the air fryer at 200°C for 3 minutes. Lightly grease the air fryer basket with cooking oil. 2. Add water to bottom of air fryer. 3. Season the steak with Montreal steak seasoning on both sides. 4. Place steak in air fryer basket, and cook 10 minutes until it reaches the doneness of medium rare, flipping the steak halfway through. 5. Transfer cooked steak to the serving plate, and top with butter halves. 6. Let rest 5 minutes, then garnish with fresh dill and serve.
Per Serving: Calories 365; Fat 23.4g; Sodium 358mg; Carbs 5.21g; Fibre 0.6g; Sugar 0.31g; Protein 33.63g

Garlicky Steak

Prep Time: 5 minutes | **Cook Time:** 8 minutes | **Serves:** 2

3 cloves garlic, peeled and minced
1 tablespoon lemon juice
1 tablespoon olive oil
½ teaspoon salt
1 (340g) strip steak

1. Combine garlic, lemon juice, olive oil, and salt in a small bowl, brush the steak with the mixture, then cover the bowl and refrigerate the steak for 30 minutes. 2. Preheat the air fryer at 200°C for 3 minutes. Lightly grease the air fryer basket with cooking oil. 3. Place the steak in air fryer basket, and cook the steak for 8 minutes until it reaches the doneness of medium rare, flipping the steak halfway through. 4. Transfer steak to a cutting board and let rest 5 minutes before slicing and serving.
Per Serving: Calories 342; Fat 15.3g; Sodium 1287mg; Carbs 2.02g; Fibre 0.1g; Sugar 0.24g; Protein 49.66g

Easy Filet Mignon

Prep Time: 5 minutes | **Cook Time:** 12 minutes | **Serves:** 2

2 (200g) filet mignon steaks, 3.8cm thick
2 teaspoons salt
1 teaspoon ground black pepper
1 tablespoon unsalted butter, cut in half

1. Preheat the air fryer at 190°C for 3 minutes. Lightly grease the air fryer basket with cooking oil. 2. Season steaks with salt and pepper on both sides. 3. Place steak in air fryer basket, and cook for 12 minutes until it reaches the doneness of medium rare, flipping the steak every 4 minutes. 4. Transfer steaks to a cutting board and top each with half of butter. 5. Let rest 5 minutes before slicing and serving.
Per Serving: Calories 321; Fat 24.84g; Sodium 2385mg; Carbs 0.93g; Fibre 0.4g; Sugar 0.01g; Protein 22.35g

Worcestershire Short Ribs

Prep Time: 10 minutes | **Cook Time:** 16 minutes | **Serves:** 2

60ml olive oil
60ml balsamic vinegar
15g chopped fresh basil leaves
15g chopped fresh oregano
⅛ teaspoon Worcestershire sauce
3 cloves garlic, peeled and quartered
½ teaspoon salt
454g beef short ribs

1. Combine olive oil, balsamic vinegar, basil, oregano, Worcestershire sauce, garlic, and salt in a large plastic resealable bag. Set aside 2 tablespoons of mixture in a small bowl. 2. Add short ribs to bag and massage mixture into ribs. Seal bag and refrigerate for 30 minutes up to overnight. 3. Preheat the air fryer at 160°C for 3 minutes. 4. Place ribs in ungreased air fryer basket, and cook for 16 minutes, flipping the ribs and brushing with extra sauce halfway through. 5. Transfer the ribs to a large serving plate, and enjoy.
Per Serving: Calories 639; Fat 47.42g; Sodium 804mg; Carbs 7.09g; Fibre 0.2g; Sugar 4.86g; Protein 46.14g

Chapter 7 Dessert Recipes

Honey Pears with Ricotta

Prep Time: 7 minutes | **Cook Time:** 18 to 23 minutes | **Serves:** 4

2 large Bosc pears, halved and seeded
3 tablespoons of honey
1 tablespoon of unsalted butter
½ teaspoon of ground cinnamon
40g o walnuts, chopped
55g of part skim low-fat ricotta cheese, divided

1. Place the pears in a suitable baking pan with cut-side up. 2. In a small microwave-safe bowl, melt the honey, butter, and cinnamon. Brush this mixture over the cut sides of the pears. 3. Pour 3 tablespoons of water around the pears in the pan, then roast the pears in the air fryer at 175°C for 18 to 23 minutes, or until tender when pierced with a fork and slightly crisp on the edges, basting once with the liquid in the pan. 4. Carefully remove the pears from the pan, and place on a serving plate. 5. Drizzle each with some liquid from the pan, sprinkle the walnuts on top, and serve with a spoonful of ricotta cheese.
Per Serving: Calories 198; Fat 7.07g; Sodium 68mg; Carbs 31.61g; Fibre 3.9g; Sugar 24.32g; Protein 3.66g

Grilled Fruit Skewers

Prep Time: 10 minutes | **Cook Time:** 3 to 5 minutes | **Serves:** 4

2 peaches, peeled, pitted, and thickly sliced
3 plums, halved and pitted
3 nectarines, halved and pitted
1 tablespoon of honey
½ teaspoon of ground cinnamon
¼ teaspoon of ground allspice
Pinch of cayenne pepper

1. Thread the fruit, alternating the types, on to 8 bamboo or metal skewers that fit into the air fryer. 2. Stir the honey, cinnamon, allspice, and cayenne in a small bowl, then brush the glaze onto the fruit. 3. Grill the skewers at 200°C for 3 to 5 minutes until lightly browned and caramelized. 4. Cool for 5 minutes and serve.
Per Serving: Calories 95; Fat 0.58g; Sodium 1mg; Carbs 23.68g; Fibre 3g; Sugar 19.4g; Protein 1.61g

Greek Peaches with Blueberries

Prep Time: 10 minutes | **Cook Time:** 7 to 11 minutes | **Serves:** 6

3 peaches, peeled, halved, and pitted
2 tablespoons of packed brown sugar
280g of plain fat-free Greek yoghurt
1 teaspoon of pure vanilla extract
¼ teaspoon of ground cinnamon
165g of fresh blueberries

1. Place the peaches in the air fryer basket with cut-side up, and evenly sprinkle them with the brown sugar. 2. Bake the peaches at 195°C for 7 to 11 minutes until they start to brown around the edges and become tender. 3. While baking the peaches, stir the yoghurt, vanilla, and cinnamon in a small bowl. 4. When the peaches are done, transfer them to a serving plate. Top with the yoghurt mixture and the blueberries. 5. Enjoy.
Per Serving: Calories 67; Fat 0.34g; Sodium 7mg; Carbs 14.25g; Fibre 1.8g; Sugar 12.06g; Protein 2.8g

Walnut-Stuffed Apples

Prep Time: 15 minutes | **Cook Time:** 12 to 17 minutes | **Serves:** 4

4 medium apples, rinsed and patted dry
2 tablespoons of freshly squeezed lemon juice
40g of golden raisins
3 tablespoons of chopped walnuts
3 tablespoons of dried cranberries

2 tablespoons of packed brown sugar
80ml of apple cider

1 Peel the apples and remove the core, being careful not to cut through the bottom of the apple. 2. Sprinkle the cut parts of the apples with lemon juice and place in a suitable pan. 3. Mix the raisins, walnuts, cranberries, and brown sugar in a small bowl, then stuff one-fourth of this mixture into each apple. 4. Pour the apple cider around the apples in the pan. 5. Bake the stuffed apples at 175°C for 12 to 17 minutes the apples are tender when pierced with a fork. 6.Serve immediately.
Per Serving: Calories 195; Fat 3.88g; Sodium 4mg; Carbs 42.33g; Fibre 5.2g; Sugar 32.56g; Protein 2.28g

Honey Apple-Peach Crisp

Prep Time: 10 minutes | **Cook Time:** 10 to 12 minutes | **Serves:** 4
1 apple, peeled and chopped
2 peaches, peeled, pitted, and chopped
2 tablespoons of honey
40g of quick-cooking oatmeal
40g of wholewheat pastry flour
3 tablespoons of packed brown sugar
2 tablespoons of unsalted butter, at room temperature
½ teaspoon of ground cinnamon

1. Thoroughly mix the apple, peaches, and honey in a suitable baking pan. 2. Mix the oatmeal, pastry flour, brown sugar, butter, and cinnamon in a medium bowl until crumbly, then sprinkle this mixture over the fruit. 3. Bake them at 195°C for 10 to 12 minutes until the fruit is bubbly and the topping is golden brown. 4. Serve warm.
Per Serving: Calories 209; Fat 5.2g; Sodium 49mg; Carbs 39.94g; Fibre 3.9g; Sugar 27.02g; Protein 3.9g

Strawberry Crumble

Prep Time: 10 minutes | **Cook Time:** 12 to 17 minutes | **Serves:** 6
190g of sliced fresh strawberries
90g of sliced rhubarb
65g of sugar
80g of quick-cooking oatmeal
60g of wholewheat pastry flour
40g of packed brown sugar
½ teaspoon of ground cinnamon
3 tablespoons of unsalted butter, melted

1. Combine the strawberries, rhubarb, and sugar in a suitable baking pan. 2. Mix the oatmeal, pastry flour, brown sugar, and cinnamon in a medium bowl. 3. Stir the melted butter into the oatmeal mixture until crumbly, then sprinkle this over the fruit. 4. Bake them at 185°C for 12 to 17 minutes until the fruit is bubbling and the topping is golden brown. 5. Serve warm.
Per Serving: Calories 168; Fat 4.99g; Sodium 47mg; Carbs 29.3g; Fibre 2.6g; Sugar 17.55g; Protein 3.31g

Berries Crumble

Prep Time: 10 minutes | **Cook Time:** 11 to 16 minutes | **Serves:** 4
65g of chopped fresh strawberries
85g of fresh blueberries
45g of frozen raspberries
1 tablespoon of freshly squeezed lemon juice
1 tablespoon of honey
80g of wholewheat pastry flour
3 tablespoons of packed brown sugar
2 tablespoons of unsalted butter, melted

1. Combine the strawberries, blueberries, and raspberries in a suitable baking pan, then drizzle them with the lemon juice and honey. 2. Mix the pastry flour and brown sugar in a small bowl, then stir in the butter and mix until crumbly. 3. Sprinkle this mixture over the fruit. 4. Bake them at 195°C for 11 to 16 minutes until the fruit is tender and bubbly

and the topping is golden brown. 5. Serve warm.

Per Serving: Calories 183; Fat 4.6g; Sodium 5mg; Carbs 34.86g; Fibre 3.8g; Sugar 18.3g; Protein 3.38g

Apple-Blueberry Pies

Prep Time: 20 minutes | **Cook Time:** 10 minutes | **Serves:** 4

1 medium Granny Smith apple, peeled and finely chopped
60g of dried blueberries
1 tablespoon of freshly squeezed orange juice
1 tablespoon of packed brown sugar
2 teaspoons of cornflour
4 sheets of frozen filo dough, thawed
8 teaspoons of unsalted butter, melted
8 teaspoons of sugar
Non-stick cooking spray, for coating the filo dough

1. Combine the apple, blueberries, orange juice, brown sugar, and cornflour in a medium bowl. 2. Place a sheet of filo dough on a work surface with the narrow side facing you, lightly brush with 1 teaspoon of butter and sprinkle with 1 teaspoon of sugar. 3. Fold the filo sheet in half from left to right, and place ¼ of the fruit filling at the bottom of the sheet in the centre. 4. Fold the left side of the sheet over the filling, and lightly spray with cooking spray, fold the right side of the sheet over the filling, and then brush with 1 teaspoon of butter and sprinkle with 1 teaspoon of sugar. 5. Fold the bottom right corner of the dough up to meet the left side of the pastry sheet to form a triangle. Continue folding the triangles over to enclose the filling, as you would fold a flag. 6. Seal the edge with a bit of water, and lightly spray with cooking spray. 7. Do the same the remaining 3 sheets of the filo, butter, sugar, and cooking spray, making four pies. 8. Place the pies in the air fryer basket, and then bake them at 200°C for 7 to 9 minutes, until golden brown and

crisp. 9. Remove the pies and let cool on a wire rack before serving.

Per Serving: Calories 225; Fat 6.88g; Sodium 96mg; Carbs 40.32g; Fibre 3.1g; Sugar 24.71g; Protein 2.37g

Oatmeal-Carrot Cups

Prep Time: 10 minutes | **Cook Time:** 8 to 10 minutes | **Serves:** 16

3 tablespoons of unsalted butter, at room temperature
45g of packed brown sugar
1 tablespoon of honey
1 egg white
½ teaspoon of vanilla extract
55g of finely grated carrot
40g of quick-cooking oatmeal
40g of wholewheat pastry flour
½ teaspoon of baking soda
30g of dried cherries

1. Beat the butter, brown sugar, and honey in a small bowl until well combined, then mix in the egg white, vanilla, and carrot. 2. Stir in the oatmeal, pastry flour, and baking soda. 3. Stir in the dried cherries. 4. Double up 32 mini muffin foil cups to make 16 cups. Fill each with about 4 teaspoons of dough. 5. Working in batches, bake the muffin cups at 175°C for 8 to 10 minutes, until light golden brown and just set. 6. Serve warm.

Per Serving: Calories 50; Fat 1.73g; Sodium 58mg; Carbs 7.94g; Fibre 0.5g; Sugar 5.22g; Protein 1.08g

Dark Chocolate Cookies

Prep Time: 10 minutes | **Cook Time:** 8 to 13 minutes | **Serves:** 30

3 tablespoons of unsalted butter
55g of dark chocolate, chopped
90g of packed brown sugar
2 egg whites
1 teaspoon of pure vanilla extract
80g of quick-cooking oatmeal
60g of wholewheat pastry flour

½ teaspoon of baking soda
30g of dried cranberries

1. Mix the butter and dark chocolate in a medium oven-safe bowl. 2. Bake them in the air fryer at 160°C for 1 to 3 minutes until the butter and chocolate melt, then stir until smooth. 3. Beat in the brown sugar, egg whites, and vanilla until smooth. 4. Stir in the oatmeal, pastry flour, and baking soda. 5. Stir in the cranberries, then form the dough into about 30 25mm balls. 6. Working in batches, bake the dough balls in the air fryer basket at 160°C for 7 to 10 minutes until set. 7. Carefully remove the cookies from the air fryer and cool on a wire rack. 8. Serve and enjoy.
Per Serving: Calories 52; Fat 1.87g; Sodium 39mg; Carbs 7.96g; Fibre 0.6g; Sugar 5.1g; Protein 1.11g

Vanilla Lava Cakes

Prep Time: 10 minutes | **Cook Time:** 10 minutes | **Serves:** 3

2 large eggs
1 teaspoon vanilla extract
¼ teaspoon salt
3 tablespoons unsalted butter
125g milk chocolate chips
30g plain flour

1. Preheat the air fryer to 175°C. Spray three suitable ramekins with cooking spray. 2. Whisk eggs, vanilla, and salt in a medium bowl until well combined. 3. Add butter and chocolate to a large microwave-safe bowl, and microwave them in 20-second intervals, stirring after each interval, until mixture is fully melted, smooth, and pourable. 4. Whisk chocolate and slowly add egg mixture until fully combined. 5. Sprinkle flour into bowl and whisk into chocolate mixture until easily pourable. 6. Divide batter evenly among prepared ramekins. 7. Place in the air fryer basket and cook for 5 minutes until the edges and top are set. 8. Let them cool for 5

minutes and use a butter knife to loosen the edges from ramekins. 9. Place a small dessert plate upside down on top of each ramekin. Quickly flip ramekin and plate upside down so lava cake drops to the plate. 10. Let them cool for 5 minutes. Enjoy.
Per Serving: Calories 204; Fat 11.61g; Sodium 285mg; Carbs 16.25g; Fibre 0.6g; Sugar 6.54g; Protein 7.75g

Cinnamon Pretzel Bites

Prep Time: 15 minutes | **Cook Time:** 1 hour 10 minutes | **Serves:** 4

125g plain flour
1 teaspoon quick-rise yeast
2 tablespoons granulated sugar, divided
¼ teaspoon salt
1 tablespoon olive oil
80ml warm water
2 teaspoons baking soda
1 teaspoon ground cinnamon

1. Mix flour, yeast, 2 teaspoons sugar, and salt in a large bowl until combined. 2. Pour in oil and water and stir until a dough begins to form and pull away from the edges of the bowl. Remove dough from the bowl and transfer to a lightly floured surface. Knead 10 minutes until dough is mostly smooth. 3. Spritz dough with cooking spray and place into a large clean bowl. Cover with plastic wrap and let rise for 1 hour. 4. Preheat the air fryer to 200°C. 5. Press dough into a suitable rectangle. Cut dough into twenty-four even pieces. 6. Fill a medium saucepan over medium-high heat halfway with water and bring to a boil. Add baking soda and let it boil 1 minute, then add pretzel bites. 7. Cook them for 45 seconds, then remove from water and drain. They will be puffy but should have mostly maintained their shape. 8. Spritz pretzel bites with cooking spray. Place in the air fryer basket and cook for 5 minutes until golden brown. 9. Mix remaining sugar and cinnamon in a small bowl. When pretzel bites

are done cooking, immediately toss in cinnamon and sugar mixture. Enjoy.

Per Serving: Calories 164; Fat 3.7g; Sodium 820mg; Carbs 28.67g; Fibre 1.3g; Sugar 4.03g; Protein 3.61g

Homemade Brownies

Prep Time: 5 minutes | **Cook Time:** 20 minutes | **Serves:** 8

65g plain flour
190g granulated sugar
20g cocoa powder
½ teaspoon baking powder
6 tablespoons salted butter, melted
1 large egg
85g semisweet chocolate chips

1. Preheat the air fryer to 175°C. Generously grease two suitable round cake pans. 2. Combine the flour, sugar, cocoa powder, and baking powder in a large bowl. 3. Add butter, egg, and chocolate chips to dry ingredients, and stir them until well combined. 4. Apportion the batter between prepared pans. 5. Place them in the air fryer basket and cook for 20 minutes until a toothpick inserted into the centre comes out clean. 6. Let them cool for 5 minutes before serving.

Per Serving: Calories 187; Fat 9.83g; Sodium 15mg; Carbs 23.44g; Fibre 1.8g; Sugar 14.02g; Protein 2.98g

Chocolate Doughnut Holes

Prep Time: 10 minutes | **Cook Time:** 22 minutes | **Serves:** 5

130g self-rising flour
305g plain full-fat Greek yogurt
20g cocoa powder
95g granulated sugar
120g icing sugar
60g heavy cream
1 teaspoon vanilla extract

1. Preheat the air fryer to 175°C. Spray the inside of the air fryer basket with cooking spray. 2. In a large bowl, combine flour, yogurt, cocoa powder, and granulated sugar. Knead by hand 5 minutes until a large, sticky ball of dough is formed. 3. Roll mixture into balls, about 2 tablespoons each, to make twenty doughnut holes. Place doughnut holes in the air fryer basket, and cook for 12 minutes, working in batches as necessary. 4. While doughnut holes are cooking, mix icing sugar, cream, and vanilla in a medium bowl. 5. Allow doughnut holes to cool for 5 minutes before rolling each in the glaze, then chill in the refrigerator 5 minutes to allow glaze to set before serving.

Per Serving: Calories 276; Fat 3.98g; Sodium 345mg; Carbs 55.58g; Fibre 2g; Sugar 34.06g; Protein 6.59g

Lemon Bars

Prep Time: 10 minutes | **Cook Time:** 20 minutes | **Serves:** 8

6 tablespoons salted butter, softened
140g granulated sugar, divided
1 teaspoon vanilla extract
125g plus 2 tablespoons plain flour, divided
60ml lemon juice
2 large eggs
1 teaspoon lemon zest

1. Preheat the air fryer to 175°C. Spray a suitable round cake pan with cooking spray. 2. Mix butter and 45 g sugar in a large bowl. 3. Stir in vanilla and 125 g flour, press this mixture into prepared pan and place in the air fryer basket. 4. Cook them in the air fryer for 5 minutes until golden brown. 4. Mix the remaining sugar, lemon juice, eggs, remaining 2 tablespoons flour, and lemon zest in a separate bowl. 5. Pour mixture over baked crust and return to the air fryer to cook for 15 minutes. 6. Let cool completely before cutting into eight sections and serving.

Per Serving: Calories 165; Fat 7.08g; Sodium 65mg; Carbs 22.01g; Fibre 0.4g; Sugar 9.54g; Protein 3.27g

Vanilla Chocolate Chip Cookies

Prep Time: 5 minutes | **Cook Time:** 20 minutes | **Serves:** 12

55g salted butter, melted
110g brown sugar
125g plain flour
1 large egg
1 teaspoon baking powder
1 teaspoon vanilla extract
55g semisweet chocolate chips

1. Stir the butter, brown sugar, flour, egg, baking powder, and vanilla in a large bowl. 2. Gently fold in chocolate chips. Chill dough in refrigerator for 10 minutes. 3. Preheat the air fryer to 175°C. Line the air fryer basket with parchment paper. 4. Scoop the batter into portions to make twelve 5cm balls, then place them on parchment paper in the air fryer basket 5cm apart, and cook for 10 minutes until golden brown on the edges and bottom. 5. Serve warm.
Per Serving: Calories 147; Fat 7.01g; Sodium 46mg; Carbs 20.28g; Fibre 0.6g; Sugar 11.57g; Protein 1.57g

Golden Peanut Butter Cookies

Prep Time: 10 minutes | **Cook Time:** 10 minutes | **Serves:** 9

255g creamy peanut butter
220g brown sugar
55g unsalted butter, melted
2 large eggs
250g plain flour
1½ teaspoons baking powder

1. Preheat the air fryer to 160°C. Line the air fryer basket with parchment paper. 2. Combine the peanut butter and brown sugar in a large bowl; add butter and eggs, stirring until smooth. 3. Mix flour and baking powder in a medium bowl; slowly add flour mixture to peanut butter mixture, about a third at a time. Fold in to combine. 4. Roll dough into balls, about 2 tablespoons each, to make eighteen balls. 5. Place on parchment 5cm apart in the air fryer, working in batches as necessary, and cook for 10 minutes until the edges are golden brown. 6. Let them cool for 5 minutes before serving.
Per Serving: Calories 390; Fat 19.07g; Sodium 195mg; Carbs 44.16g; Fibre 2.4g; Sugar 13.95g; Protein 12.96g

Snickerdoodles

Prep Time: 10 minutes | **Cook Time:** 10 minutes | **Serves:** 18

55g unsalted butter, melted
3 tablespoons granulated sugar, divided
125g plain flour
½ teaspoon baking powder
½ teaspoon cream of tartar
1 teaspoon ground cinnamon

1. Preheat the air fryer to 160°C. Cut four pieces of parchment to fit the air fryer basket, one for each batch. 2. Mix butter and 2 tablespoons of sugar in a medium bowl. 3. In a large bowl, mix flour, baking powder, and cream of tartar. Add butter mixture to dry ingredients and stir to form dough. 4. Roll dough into balls, about 2 tablespoons each, to make eighteen balls. 5. In a small bowl, mix remaining 1 tablespoon sugar and cinnamon. Roll each ball in sugar mixture. 6. Place them on parchment in the air fryer basket 5cm apart, and cook for 10 minutes per batch until the edges are golden brown and a toothpick inserted into the centre comes out clean. 7. Let them cool for 5 minutes before serving.
Per Serving: Calories 62; Fat 3.5g; Sodium 3mg; Carbs 6.86g; Fibre 0.3g; Sugar 1.33g; Protein 0.93g

Almond-Shortbread Cookies

Prep Time: 10 minutes | **Cook Time:** 1 hour 10 minutes | **Serves:** 8

112g salted butter, softened
50g granulated sugar
1 teaspoon almond extract

1 teaspoon vanilla extract
500g plain flour

1. Cream the butter, sugar, and extracts in a large bowl, then gradually add the flour, mixing until well combined. 2. Roll the dough into a 12" x 2" log and wrap in cling film. Chill the dough in the fridge for at least 1 hour. 3. Preheat the air fryer to 300°F/ 150°C. 4. Slice dough into ¼"-thick cookies. Place in the air fryer basket 2" apart, working in batches as needed, and cook for 10 minutes until the edges start to brown. 5. Let cool completely before serving.
Per Serving: Calories 196; Fat 8.04g; Sodium 63mg; Carbs 27.07g; Fiber 0.9g; Sugar 3.22g; Protein 3.34g

Peach Oat Crumble

Prep Time: 10 minutes | **Cook Time:** 10 minutes | **Serves:** 6

64g plain flour
39g quick-cooking oats
4 tablespoons cold salted butter, cubed
¼ teaspoon salt
2 teaspoons ground cinnamon, divided
67g brown sugar, divided
1 (414g) can peaches, drained and rinsed

1. Preheat the air fryer to 350°F/ 175°C. 2. Add the flour, oats, butter, salt, 1 teaspoon of the cinnamon, and 3 tablespoons of brown sugar to a food processor. Pulse them for 15 times until large crumbs form. 3. Place the peaches in a suitable round baking dish, and sprinkle with the remaining cinnamon and brown sugar. Stir to coat the peaches. 4. Completely cover the peaches with the flour mixture, leaving larger crumbs intact as much as possible, and spray with cooking spray. 5. Place in the air fryer basket and cook for 10 minutes until the top is golden brown. 6. Serve warm.
Per Serving: Calories 165; Fat 5.52g; Sodium 142mg; Carbs 28.27g; Fiber 1.9g; Sugar 17.6g; Protein 2.05g

Simple Vanilla Cheesecake

Prep Time: 10 minutes | **Cook Time:** 20 minutes | **Serves:** 8

6 digestive biscuits
2 tablespoons salted butter, melted
354g full-fat cream cheese, softened
100g granulated sugar
2 tablespoons sour cream
1 teaspoon vanilla extract
1 large egg

1. Preheat the air fryer to 300°F/ 150°C. 2. Pulse the biscuits in a food processor for 15 minutes until finely crushed. Transfer crumbs to a medium bowl. 3. Add the butter and mix until the texture is sand-like. Press into a suitable round spring-form tin. 4. Combine cream cheese and sugar in a large bowl, stirring until no lumps remain. Mix in the sour cream and vanilla until smooth, then gently mix in egg. 5. Pour the batter over the biscuit base in the tin. Place the tin in the air fryer basket and cook for 20 minutes, until top is golden brown. 6. Chill the cheesecake in the fridge for at least 4 hours to set before serving.
Per Serving: Calories 190; Fat 10.51g; Sodium 231mg; Carbs 18.76g; Fiber 0.4g; Sugar 11.48g; Protein 5g

Chocolate Cheesecake

Prep Time: 10 minutes | **Cook Time:** 4 hours 20 minutes | **Serves:** 8

354g full-fat cream cheese, softened
100g granulated sugar
2 tablespoons sour cream
2 tablespoons cocoa powder
80g semisweet chocolate chips, melted
1 teaspoon vanilla extract
1 large egg

1. Preheat the air fryer to 300°F/ 150°C. Line a suitable round cake tin with baking paper, and spray with cooking spray. 2. Combine cream cheese and sugar in a large bowl until

no lumps remain. 3. Mix in sour cream, cocoa powder, chocolate chips, and vanilla until well combined and smooth. Stir in egg. Pour into prepared tin. 4. Place the tin in the air fryer basket and cook for 20 minutes until the top of cheesecake is firm. 5. Chill the cheesecake in the fridge for at least 4 hours to set before serving.

Per Serving: Calories 179; Fat 10.83g; Sodium 166mg; Carbs 17.71g; Fiber 1g; Sugar 14.6g; Protein 4.93g

Cheese Pound Cake

Prep Time: 10 minutes | **Cook Time:** 25 minutes | **Serves:** 8

687g plain flour
1 teaspoon baking powder
112g salted butter, melted
119g full-fat cream cheese, softened
200g granulated sugar
2 teaspoons vanilla extract
3 large eggs

1. Preheat the air fryer to 300°F/ 150°C. Spray a suitable round cake tin with cooking spray. 2. Mix flour and baking powder in a large bowl. 3. In a separate large bowl, mix butter, cream cheese, sugar, and vanilla. 4. Stir the wet ingredients into the dry ingredients, and add eggs one at a time, making sure each egg is fully incorporated before adding the next. 5. Pour the batter into the prepared tin, and then place the tin in the air fryer basket. 6. Cook the cake for 25 minutes until a toothpick inserted into the center comes out clean. If the cake begins to brown too quickly, cover the tin with foil and cut two slits in the top of foil to encourage heat circulation. Be sure to tuck foil under the bottom of the tin to ensure the air fryer fan does not blow it off. 7. Allow the cake to cool completely before serving.

Per Serving: Calories 261; Fat 11.84g; Sodium 141mg; Carbs 32.08g; Fiber 0.6g; Sugar 13.32g; Protein 5.97g

Cinnamon Apple Fritters

Prep Time: 10 minutes | **Cook Time:** 15 minutes | **Serves:** 6

125g self-rising flour
100g granulated sugar
1½ teaspoons ground cinnamon
59ml whole milk
1 large egg
118g diced Granny Smith apples

1. Preheat the air fryer to 375°F/ 190°C. Line the air fryer basket with baking paper. 2. Combine flour, sugar, cinnamon, and milk in a large bowl, then stir in the egg and gently fold in the apples. 3. Scoop dough in 6 even portions onto parchment paper. 4. Cook them for 15 minutes until golden brown and a toothpick inserted into the center comes out clean. Turning halfway through cooking time. 5. Let the fritters cool for 5 minutes before serving.

Per Serving: Calories 139; Fat 1.35g; Sodium 265mg; Carbs 28.15g; Fiber 1.4g; Sugar 11.29g; Protein 3.52g

Vanilla Pumpkin Pie

Prep Time: 5 minutes | **Cook Time:** 2 hours 25 minutes | **Serves:** 6

1 (425g) can pumpkin pie mix
1 large egg
1 teaspoon vanilla extract
80ml sweetened condensed milk
1 (170g) premade pie crust

1. Preheat the air fryer to 325°F/ 160°C. 2. Combine the pumpkin pie mix, egg, vanilla, and sweetened condensed milk in a large bowl. Pour the mixture into the pie crust. 3. Place them in the air fryer basket and cook for 25 minutes until the pie is brown, firm, and a toothpick inserted into the center comes out clean. 4. Chill in the fridge until set, for at least 2 hours, before serving.

Per Serving: Calories 240; Fat 7.76g; Sodium 162mg; Carbs 42.2g; Fiber 5.1g; Sugar 10.01g; Protein 4.98g

Peanut Cookies

Prep Time: 10 minutes | **Cook Time:** 15 minutes | **Serves:** 8

112g salted butter, melted
50g granulated sugar
1 teaspoon vanilla extract
125g plain flour
125g peanuts, finely chopped
250g icing sugar

1. Preheat the air fryer to 300°F/ 150°C. 2. Combine the butter, sugar, and vanilla in a large bowl, then gradually add the flour and the peanuts. Mix until well combined. 3. Form the dough into sixteen 1" balls. Place them in the air fryer basket, working in batches as necessary. 4. Cook them for 15 minutes, until cookies are golden brown and firm. 5. Let the cookies cool for 5 minutes before rolling them in icing sugar. Cool completely before serving.
Per Serving: Calories 423; Fat 20.05g; Sodium 258mg; Carbs 52.89g; Fiber 2.3g; Sugar 30.96g; Protein 11.02g

Caramel Apples

Prep Time: 10 minutes | **Cook Time:** 16 minutes | **Serves:** 4

4 medium Pink Lady apples
112g salted butter
8 soft caramel chew sweets
45g rolled oats
50g granulated sugar
1 teaspoon ground cinnamon

1. Preheat the air fryer to 350°F/ 175°C. 2. Carefully core the apples by cutting a large, deep square into the center from the top down. Scoop out the seeds and insides, leaving about one-fourth of apple intact at the bottom. 3. Add the butter to a medium microwave-safe bowl, and microwave for 30 seconds; add caramels and microwave for 15 seconds more. Stir quickly to finish melting the caramels into the butter. 4. Add oats, sugar, and cinnamon to caramel mixture, mix them until well combined and crumbly. 5. Scoop the mixture into the cored apples. Place them in the air fryer basket and cook for 15 minutes until the apples are wrinkled and softened. 6. Serve warm.
Per Serving: Calories 296; Fat 16.47g; Sodium 127mg; Carbs 43.48g; Fiber 6.6g; Sugar 25.22g; Protein 2.69g

Mayonnaise Chocolate Cake

Prep Time: 10 minutes | **Cook Time:** 25 minutes | **Serves:** 6

125g plain flour
100g granulated sugar
1 teaspoon baking powder
30g cocoa powder
230g mayonnaise
1 teaspoon vanilla extract
125ml whole milk

1. Preheat the air fryer to 300°F/ 150°C. Spray a suitable round cake tin with cooking spray. 2. Combine the flour, sugar, baking powder, and cocoa powder in a large bowl. Then stir in the mayonnaise, vanilla, and milk until thick but pourable. 3. Pour the batter into the prepared cake tin, and then place the tin in the air fryer basket. 4. Cook the cake for 25 minutes until a toothpick inserted into the center comes out clean. 5. Serve warm.
Per Serving: Calories 266; Fat 14.02g; Sodium 320mg; Carbs 30.63g; Fiber 2.1g; Sugar 11.31g; Protein 5.79g

Easy-to-Make Coconut Cupcakes

Prep Time: 10 minutes | **Cook Time:** 15 minutes | **Serves:** 12

125g plain flour
95g granulated sugar
1 teaspoon baking powder
55g salted butter, melted
1 large egg
120ml full-fat canned coconut milk
40g sweetened shredded coconut

1. Preheat the air fryer to 150°C. 2. Whisk the flour, baking powder, and sugar in a large bowl. 3. Add butter, egg, and coconut milk to dry mixture. Stir until well combined. 4. Fold in shredded coconut. Divide evenly among twelve silicone or aluminum muffin cups, filling each halfway full. 5. Place them in the air fryer basket, working in batches as necessary. Cook them for 15 minutes until brown at the edges and a toothpick inserted into the centre comes out clean. 6. Let cool for 5 minutes before serving.

Per Serving: Calories 108; Fat 5.46g; Sodium 39mg; Carbs 13.26g; Fibre 0.6g; Sugar 4.72g; Protein 1.93g

Lemon Butter Cookies

Prep Time: 10 minutes | **Cook Time:** 42 minutes | **Serves:** 4

100g full-fat cream cheese, softened
115g salted butter, softened
95g granulated sugar
1 teaspoon vanilla extract
125g plain flour
Zest and juice of 1 medium lemon plus 1 tablespoon lemon juice, divided
120g icing sugar

1. Combine cream cheese, butter, granulated sugar, and vanilla in a large bowl, then gradually add flour, lemon zest, and juice of 1 lemon. 2. Chill dough in the refrigerator for 30 minutes. While dough is chilling, mix icing' sugar with remaining 1 tablespoon lemon juice to make a glaze. 3. Preheat the air fryer to 150°C. Line the air fryer basket with parchment paper. 4. Form dough into eight 2.5cm balls. 5. Place the balls on parchment paper in the air fryer basket, working in batches as necessary, and cook them for 12 minutes until edges of the cookies are lightly brown. 6. Spoon glaze over cookies. Let them cool for 10 minutes before serving.

Per Serving: Calories 458; Fat 19.98g; Sodium 228mg; Carbs 64.54g; Fibre 0.9g; Sugar 38.86g; Protein 5.66g

Cherry Pies

Prep Time: 15 minutes | **Cook Time:** 15 minutes | **Serves:** 6

125g plain flour
115g cold salted butter, grated
5 tablespoons ice water
2 tablespoons granulated sugar
790g canned cherry pie filling
1 large egg, whisked

1. Preheat the air fryer to 160°C. Line the air fryer basket with parchment paper. 2. In a large bowl, mix flour, butter, ice water, and sugar until a soft ball of dough forms. 3. Lightly flour a work surface, roll out dough into a 30 cm × 40 cm rectangle. 4. Cut dough into six rectangles by cutting across the centre, then down into three columns. Each rectangle will be 10 cm × 20 cm. 4. Place 130 g pie filling onto the lower half of each rectangle. Fold the top over the filling and press the edges closed with a fork. 5. Gently brush top of each pie with egg. Place pies on parchment in the air fryer basket, working in batches as necessary. 6. Cook them for 15 minutes, turning after 10 minutes, until golden brown and flaky. 7. Let the pies cool for 10 minutes after cooking, then enjoy.

Per Serving: Calories 258; Fat 11.41g; Sodium 111mg; Carbs 34.44g; Fibre 2.1g; Sugar 14.78g; Protein 4.39g

Chocolate Brownies

Prep Time: 10 minutes | **Cook Time:** 11 minutes | **Serves:** 9

35g almond flour
20g unsweetened cocoa
10g sweetener
½ teaspoon baking soda
3 tablespoons unsalted butter, melted
1 tablespoon sour cream
1 large egg
⅛ teaspoon salt
40g sugar-free semisweet chocolate chips
30g chopped pecans

1. Preheat air fryer at 175°C for 3 minutes. 2. Combine flour, cocoa, sweetener, baking soda, butter, and sour cream in a medium bowl; stir in egg, salt, chocolate chips and chopped pecans, stirring until mixture is thick and sticky. 3. Press the mixture into a square cake barrel greased with cooking spray. 4. Cover pan with aluminum foil and place in air fryer basket. 5. Cook the mixture for 9 minutes. Remove foil and cook for an additional 2 minutes. 5. Remove pan from air fryer and let cool 30 minutes. Once cooled, slice into nine sections and serve.

Per Serving: Calories 98; Fat 7.75g; Sodium 128mg; Carbs 8.9g; Fibre 2.4g; Sugar 0.25g; Protein 2.35g

Giant Chocolate Cookies

Prep Time: 10 minutes | **Cook Time:** 8 minutes | **Serves:** 9

35g almond flour
2 tablespoons powdered sweetener
1 large egg
½ teaspoon vanilla extract
3 tablespoons butter, melted
⅛ teaspoon salt
2 tablespoons sugar-free dark chocolate chips

1. Preheat air fryer at 175°C for 3 minutes. 2. Combine all ingredients except chocolate chips in a medium bowl, then fold in chocolate chips. 3. Spoon mixture into a pizza pan greased with cooking spray. Place the pan in air fryer basket and cook for 8 minutes. 4. Slice and serve warm.

Per Serving: Calories 43; Fat 4.44g; Sodium 79mg; Carbs 0.67g; Fibre 0.1g; Sugar 0.06g; Protein 0.46g

Conclusion

The tower air fryer is the most versatile and advanced appliance around the world. The tower air fryer has a large capacity and is the perfect cooking appliance for whole family. It has a lot of cooking functions. You can cook everything using this air fryer. This cookbook has a lot of tower air frying recipes – step-by-step cooking instructions, easy-to-find ingredients, prep/cook time, and serving suggestions. If you want to make your life easier and more comfortable, then an air fryer is the best appliance for you. It saves your time plus money. You will get breakfast, poultry, lamb, beef, dessert, chicken, and snacks recipes from this cookbook. All recipes are delicious and easy to cook. You can select your favorite recipe from this book and start cooking after reading the instructions about this appliance. This appliance has user-friendly operating buttons and valuable accessories. You didn't need to buy a separate oven or dehydrator to bake or dehydrate food. This appliance offers all the useful functions that you need. This cooking function has a large capacity. You can prepare food for a large family. This unit is the perfect option for holidays. You can spend a lot of time with your family instead of standing in the kitchen for a long time. Prepare a quick breakfast for your kids in the morning. This appliance is perfect for those who have no time to cook for a long time. If you don't have any knowledge of using this appliance, read this cookbook thoroughly. I hope you will get all answers that come to your mind. Thank you for choosing our cookbook. I hope you like our recipes and book introduction. Thank you for appreciating us.

Appendix Recipes Index

A

Almond Salmon Fillets 54

Almond-Shortbread Cookies   92

Apple Chicken Sausage 24

Apple-Blueberry Pies   89

Artichoke Triangles 40

B

Bacon Chicken 72

Bacon Stuffed Prawns 58

Bacon with Brussels Sprouts   29

Bacon-Wrapped Jalapeño Poppers 44

Bacon-Wrapped Jalapeños 48

Bacon-Wrapped Onion Slices   49

Baked Hard Eggs   25

Baked Peaches Oatmeal   21

Baked Potato Skins 23

Baked Sweet Potatoes with Brown Sugar 36

Balsamic Asparagus   31

Banana-Nut Muffins 19

Barbecue Chicken Legs 63

BBQ Beef Bowls 76

Beef and Broccoli Bowls 76

Beef Broccoli in Stock   84

Beef Chimichangas 77

Beef Taco Meatballs   46

Beef-Stuffed Peppers   84

Berries Crumble   88

Berry Muffins   26

Blistered Peppers   34

Blue Cheese Beef Burgers 74

Bread Crumbs Fried Pickles 47

Breaded Avocado Fries 28

Breaded Bell Pepper Strips 29

Breaded Chicken Strips 65

Breaded Drumettes 61

Breaded Fish Sticks 57

Breaded Green Beans   32

Breaded Shrimp Toast 41

Breaded Thin Pork Chops   79

Broccoli Carrot Bites   48

Buffalo Chicken Bites with Blue Cheese 42

Butter Bay Scallops 56

Butter Cheese Crackers 45

Butter Ribeye Steak   85

Buttered Green Beans with Almonds   34

Buttermilk Cornish Hen 68

C

Cajun Chicken Bites   73

Cajun Salmon Fillets   50

Caramel Apples 95

Cheese Broccoli–Stuffed Chicken   69

Cheese Chicken Nuggets   72

Cheese Courgette Fritters   36

Cheese Ham Chicken   72

Cheese Portobello Pizzas   33

Cheese Pound Cake 94

Cheese Spaghetti Pie   67

Cheese-Stuffed Mushrooms 49

Cherry Pies 96

Chicken Bulgogi with Rice   61

Chicken Club Sandwiches   64

Chicken Cobb Salad 65

Chicken Parmesan Pizzadillas   66

Chicken Quesadillas   67

Chicken Satay Kebabs 63

Chili Pork Loin 79

Chipotle Chicken Wings 73

Chocolate Brownies 97

Chocolate Cheesecake 93

Chocolate Doughnut Holes 91

Cinnamon Apple Chips 48

Cinnamon Apple Fritters   94

Cinnamon Bagels   19

Cinnamon Doughnut Holes 17

Cinnamon Pretzel Bites 90

Coconut Pork Satay 80

Coriander Baked Salmon   54

Corn Beef Hot Dogs 44

Crab Cakes with Watercress Salad 57

Crab Legs with Lemon Butter Dip   51

Cranberry Beignets 27

Cream Cheese Wontons   44

Cream Chicken Patties 63

Cream Mashed Potatoes   37

Cream Prawn Scampi   52

Crisp Carrot Chips   28

Crispy Salmon Patties   51

Crunchy Potatoes   32

Crustless Broccoli Quiche   24

Curried Sweet Potato Fries 39

Curry Chicken Salad   64

D

Dark Chocolate Cookies 89

Delicious Broccoli Cheese Tots 30

Delicious Chicken Avocado Paninis 65

Delicious Firecracker Shrimp   52

Delicious Spinach Dip with Bread Knots 40

Delicious Sweet Potatoes   32

Dijon Roasted Purple Potatoes 37

E

Ears of Corn   36

Easy Buttery Cod   55

Easy Filet Mignon   86

Easy Jam Doughnuts   17

Easy Potato Chips   43

Easy Rainbow Carrots   34

Easy Raw Prawn   58

Easy-to-Make Coconut Cupcakes   96

Eggs in Tomato Sauce 23

F

Fajita Chicken Thigh Meatballs 69

Fish Fingers   51

Fish Vegetable Bowl   53

Flavorful Chicken Wings   43

Flavourful Asparagus Strata   25

Flavourful Broccoli 30

Flavourful Chicken Legs 62

Flavourful Chicken Tenders 71

Foil-Packet Lemon Salmon 51

Foil-Packet Lobster Tail with Parsley   52

Fried Tortellini with Mayonnaise 41

Fried Tuna Avocado Balls   53

G

Garlic Asparagus   34

Garlicky Steak 85

Garlicky Wings 69

Giant Chocolate Cookies   97

Ginger Chicken Thigh Pieces   72

Glazed Cinnamon Rolls 22

Glazed Pork-Apple Skewers 78

Golden Peanut Butter Cookies 92

Granola Cereal 18

Greek Chicken Salad   62

Greek Peaches with Blueberries 87

Greek Vegetable Beef Bowl 83

Grilled Fruit Skewers   87

Grilled Pork Tenderloin 82

H

Hard Boiled Eggs   19

Hash Browns   20

Healthy Butternut Squash Purée   35

Herbed Vegetable Breakfast   24

Homemade Arancini   41

Homemade Brownies   91

Homemade Mozzarella Sticks   45

Homemade Pancake   27

Homemade Veggie Burger   33

Honey Apple-Peach Crisp   88

Honey Brussels Sprouts 35

Honey Pears with Ricotta   87

Hot Chicken Wings 47

J

Jalapeño Chicken Meatballs 67

K

Kale Chips with Yoghurt Sauce 39

Korean-Style Chicken Wings   47

L

Lean Pork-Egg Rolls   46

Lemon Bars 91

Lemon Butter Cookies 96

Lemon Crab-Stuffed Mushrooms   56

Lemon Jumbo Sea Scallops 60

Lemony Chicken Meatballs 66

Lemony Shrimp 50

Light Herbed Beef Meatballs   83

Lime Tortilla Chips 44

Lime–Crusted Halibut Fillets   58

M

Mayonnaise Chocolate Cake   95

Mayonnaise Crab Cakes 54

Mini Beef Meatloaves   74

Mushroom Steak Bites 75

Mushroom-Beef Balls   75

Mustard Chicken Bites 66

Mustard Pork Tenderloin   81

O

Oat Blueberry Muffins   21

Oatmeal-Carrot Cups   89

Omelet Cups   26

P

Palatable Chipotle Drumsticks   71

Panko Breaded Pork Cutlets 78

Panko Onion Rings 43

Parmesan Beef Risotto 85

Parmesan Croutons 46

Parmesan Drumsticks   71

Parmesan Hash Brown Bruschetta   42

Peach Oat Crumble 93

Peanut Banana Loaf   22

Peanut Cookies 95

Pecan-Crusted Chicken 71

Pepper & Onion Hash   20

Pesto Bruschetta   41

Pesto Chicken Pizzas   69

Pickle-Brined Chicken   70

Pineapple Pork Sliders   80

Pork and Salad 80

Pork Cabbage Burgers   81

Pork Meatball Bowl 79

Pork Rind Fried Chicken 70

Pork Tenderloin with Apple Slices   81

Pork Tenderloin with Potatoes   82

Pork-Fruit Kebabs   82

Prawn Frittata   26

Prawn-Vegetable Kebabs   55

Prep Day Chicken Breasts   61

Puffed Egg Tarts   20

Q

Quiche 21

R

Raisin Granola Bars 18

Red Hassel-backs   37

Roasted Broccoli   30

Roasted Cauliflower 31

Roasted Tomatoes 29

Russet Potato Skins 46

S

Salmon Cakes with Special Sauce   59

Salmon Jerky   55

Salsa Verde Chicken   61

Savory Wings   68

Scrambled Eggs   19

Sesame Carrots35

Sesame Tuna Steak   54

Simple Fried Broccoli   35

Simple Green Beans and Potatoes   32

Simple Grilled Steaks   83

Simple Rib Eye Steak   78

Simple Roasted Shallots   35

Simple Vanilla Cheesecake   93

Sirloin Steak and Eggs   25

Sirloin Steak Roll-Ups   77

Smoked Salmon with Baked Avocados   59

Smoky Calamari Rings   56

Snickerdoodles   92

Special Beef-Mango Skewers   39

Spiced Chicken Thighs   70

Spiced Crab Dip   53

Spiced Pork Chops   79

Spiced Shrimp   50

Spicy Corn on Cob   29

Spicy Pickle Fries   28

Spinach-Cheese–Stuffed Mushrooms   31

Steak-Vegetable Kebabs   82

Steak-Veggie Kebabs   75

Stir-Fried Beef and Fruit   84

Strawberry Crumble   88

Stuffed Bell Peppers   74

Super Easy Pepperoni Chips   49

T

Tasty Coconut Shrimps 50

Tasty Pot Stickers   39

Tasty Scotch Eggs   26

Tasty Steak Fingers77

Tasty Steamer Clams   56

Toast Sticks   17

Toaster Pastries   18

Tuna Courgette Casserole   52

Tuna Croquettes with Dill   58

Tuna on Tomatoes   59

Turkey Meatballs   45

Twice-Baked Potatoes   38

V

Vanilla Chocolate Chip Cookies 92

Vanilla Lava Cakes   90

Vanilla Pumpkin Pie94

W

Waffle Fry Poutine   42

Walnut-Stuffed Apples   87

Whole-Wheat Bagels   22

Worcestershire Short Ribs   86

Printed in Great Britain
by Amazon

13908309R00059